Getting Started with Enterprise Miner™ Software, Release 4.1

SAS Publishing

The Power to Know™

The correct bibliographic citation for this manual is as follows: SAS Institute Inc., *Getting Started with Enterprise Miner™ Software, Release 4.1*, Cary, NC: SAS Institute Inc., 2000.

Getting Started with Enterprise Miner™ Software, Release 4.1

SAS Institute Inc., SAS Campus Drive, Cary, North Carolina 27513.

1st printing, October 2000

Contents

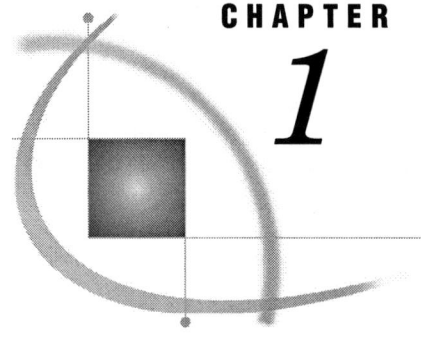

CHAPTER

1

Introduction to Enterprise Miner Software

Data Mining Overview

SAS defines *data mining* as the process of *S*electing, *E*xploring, *M*odifying, *M*odeling, and *A*ssessing (SEMMA) large amounts of data to uncover previously unknown patterns that can be utilized as a business advantage. The data mining process is applicable across a variety of industries and provides methodologies for such diverse business problems as fraud detection, householding, customer retention and attrition, database marketing, market segmentation, risk analysis, affinity analysis, customer satisfaction, bankruptcy prediction, and portfolio analysis.

Enterprise Miner software is an integrated product that provides an end-to-end business solution for data mining. A graphical user interface (GUI) provides a user-friendly front end to the SEMMA data mining process:

□ *Sample* the data by creating one or more data tables. The sample should be large enough to contain the significant information, yet small enough to process.

□ *Explore* the data by searching for anticipated relationships, unanticipated trends, and anomalies in order to gain understanding and ideas.

□ *Modify* the data by creating, selecting, and transforming the variables to focus the model selection process.

□ *Model* the data by using the analytical tools to search for a combination of the data that reliably predicts a desired outcome.

□ *Assess* the data by evaluating the usefulness and reliability of the findings from the data mining process.

You may or may not include all of these steps in your analysis, and it may be necessary to repeat one or more of the steps several times before you are satisfied with the results. After you have completed the assess phase of the SEMMA process, you apply the scoring formula from one or more champion models to new data that may or may not contain the target. Scoring new data that is not available at the time of model training is the end result of most data mining problems.

The SEMMA data mining process is driven by a process flow diagram, which you can modify and save. The GUI is designed in such a way that the business analyst who has little statistical expertise can navigate through the data mining methodology, while the quantitative expert can go "behind the scenes" to fine-tune the analytical process.

Enterprise Miner contains a collection of sophisticated analysis tools that have a common user-friendly interface that you can use to create and compare multiple models. Statistical tools include clustering, self-organizing maps / Kohonen, variable selection, trees, linear and logistic regression, and neural networking. Data preparation tools include outlier detection, variable transformations, data imputation, random sampling, and the partitioning of data sets (into train, test, and validate data sets). Advanced visualization tools enable you to quickly and easily examine large amounts of data in multidimensional histograms and to graphically compare modeling results.

This documentation describes the core functionality of Enterprise Miner and shows you how to perform basic tasks. For more detail on the individual tool nodes, see the online Enterprise Miner Reference Help documentation that is available from the main menu:

| Help | ▶ | Enterprise Miner Reference |

Enterprise Miner is designed for PCs that are running Windows 95/98, Windows NT 4.0, or subsequent releases of those operating environments. The screen captures presented in this document were taken on a PC running Windows NT 4.0.

Layout of Enterprise Miner

To start Enterprise Miner, start up SAS and then type **miner** in the command dialog box of the SAS Display Manager. The SAS Enterprise Miner window opens:

The SAS Enterprise Miner v.4 Window

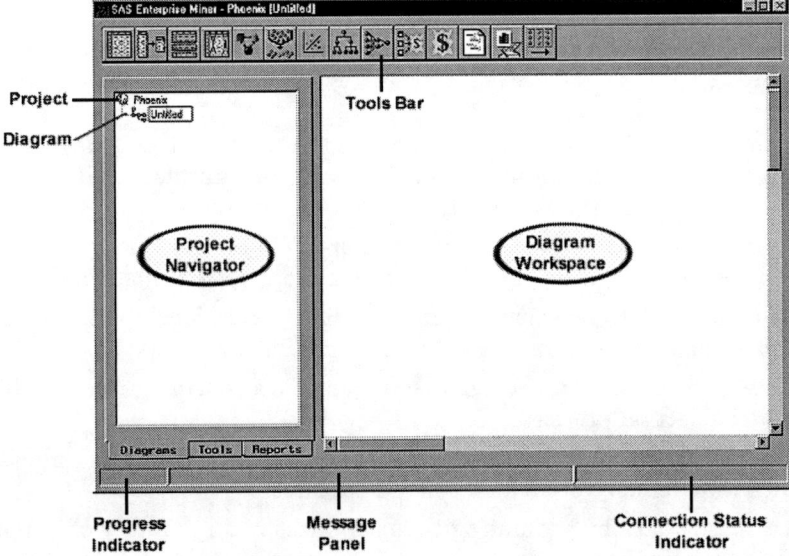

The SAS Enterprise Miner window contains the following interface components:

☐ *Project Navigator* — You use the Project Navigator to manage projects and diagrams, add tools to the Diagram Workspace, and view HTML reports that are created by the *Reporter* node. Note that once a tool is added to the Diagram Workspace, it is referred to as a node. The Project Navigator has three tabs:

□ Diagram tab — lists the current project and the diagrams within the project. By default, Enterprise Miner creates a local project that uses your userid as the name (for this example, **Phoenix**) and a process flow diagram named **Untitled**. When you re–open Enterprise Miner, the last project you were working with is loaded.

□ Tools tab — contains the Enterprise Miner tools pallet. The tools pallet presents all the data mining tools that are available for constructing process flow diagrams. The tools are grouped according to the SEMMA data mining methodology.

□ Reports tab — contains the HTML report entries for the project. You generate reports using Enterprise Miner's *Reporter* node.

□ *Diagram Workspace* — enables you to build, edit, run, and save process flow diagrams.

□ *Tools Bar* — contains a customizable subset of Enterpriser Miner tools that are commonly used to build process flow diagrams in the Diagram Workspace. You can add or delete tools from the Tools Bar.

□ *Progress Indicator* — displays a progress indicator bar that indicates the execution status of an Enterprise Miner task.

□ *Message Panel* — displays messages about the execution of an Enterprise Miner task.

□ *Connection Status Indicator* — displays the remote host name and indicates whether or not the connection is active for a client/server project.

Using the Application Main Menus

You use Enterprise Miner's application menus to quickly and efficiently perform common tasks. Different windows have different menus. Here is a brief summary of the SAS Enterprise Miner window pull-down menus:

□ **File**

□ **New**

□ **Project** — creates a new project.

□ **Diagram** — creates a new diagram.

□ **Open** — opens a new or existing diagram within the current project.

□ **Import Version 2 project** — imports an Enterprise Miner 2.0x project.

□ **Save Diagram** — saves the current diagram to the project.

□ **Save Diagram as** — names and saves the current diagram to the project.

□ **Print Setup** — specifies printing options.

□ **Print** — prints the contents of the SAS Enterprise Miner window.

□ **Delete current project** — deletes the current project. If you select this menu item, then a message appears that asks you to verify the deletion.

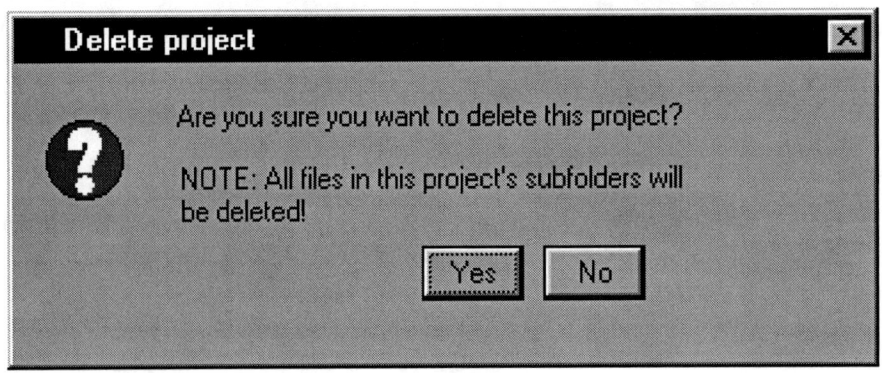

To delete the project, select Yes. All files in the project folder and any subfolders will be deleted. If you select No, then the project is not deleted. You cannot delete a project that someone else has opened.

☐ **Close diagram** — closes and saves the diagram.

☐ **Close project** — closes the project.

☐ **Exit Enterprise Miner** — ends the Enterprise Miner session.

☐ **Edit**

☐ **Copy diagram to clipboard** — copies the diagram to the clipboard.

☐ **Undelete** — undeletes the last deleted node.

☐ **Copy** — copies a node or object to the paste buffer. You must first select the node or object you want to copy.

☐ **Delete** — deletes the selected node or connection from the Diagram Workspace.

☐ **Clone** — clones the selected node (copies the current node and adds it to the Custom folder of the Tools Palette).

☐ **Paste** — pastes the node, diagram, or object from the clipboard.

☐ **Select all** — selects all nodes in the Diagram Workspace.

☐ **Create subdiagram** — creates a subdiagram that you use to collapse a set of selected nodes and connections into a single *Subdiagram* node icon.

☐ **View**

☐ **Messages** — opens the Messages window that displays collected messages for this diagram.

Use the window control buttons to close the Messages window.

☐ **Refresh** — refreshes the Project Navigator and the Diagram Workspace view.

☐ **Up One Level** — displays the next higher level of the process flow diagram. If there are no subdiagrams in your process flow diagram, then only one level can be displayed. If there are subdiagrams in your process flow diagram, then the subdiagrams can be displayed either in their condensed form (hiding the internal structure of the subdiagram) or in their expanded form (showing their internal structure). The higher level displays subdiagrams in condensed form.

□ **Top Level** — displays the process flow diagram in its most condensed form. All subdiagrams are condensed.

□ **Options**

    □ **User preferences** — opens the User Preferences window that enables you to specify startup options, set the default directories for new projects, set up server profiles for client/server projects, and specify the HTML report items that you want to display when you run the *Reporter* node.

After making your selections in the User Preferences window, select OK.

□ **Projects**

    □ **Data Profiles** — opens the Data Profile window that you use to define target profile information for a data set. To learn about defining target profiles, read the Target Profiler chapter in the online Enterprise Miner Reference, available from the application's main Help menu.

    After making your selections in the Data Profile window, close the window and save your changes.

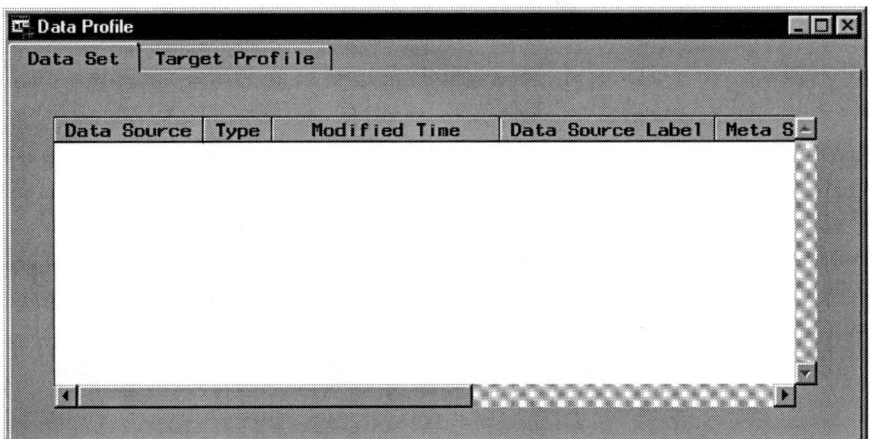

☐ **Properties** — shows project properties, such as the project name and type, share status, project location, server information, and a list of users that have the project open. You can also specify start-up and exit code that runs when the project is opened and closed, specify the SAS warehouse path, or update the project server profile. These settings can be specified if the project is opened by one user.

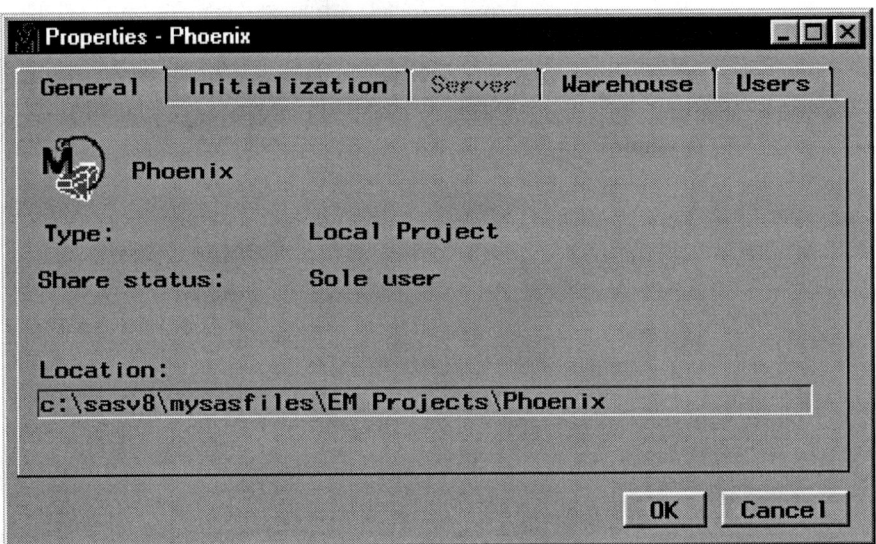

☐ **Diagram**

☐ **Connect items** — a mode of editing where node icons are fixed in location, so that you can more easily make connections among them.

☐ **Move items** — a mode of editing where node icons cannot be connected, so that you may more easily move the icons into desired locations in the process flow diagram.

☐ **Move and Connect** — (default) a mode of editing where node icons can be moved and connected in the Diagram Workspace.

☐ **Large icons** — displays large node icons in the Diagram Workspace. This item is grayed out if a node is selected in the Diagram Workspace.

☐ **Small icons** — (default) displays small node icons in the Diagram Workspace. This item is grayed out if a node is selected in the Diagram Workspace.

☐ **Properties** — opens the Properties window that enables you to view diagram properties, such as the name, type, status, date created, and date last modified. You can also password protect a diagram in the Protection tab and type and store notes about the diagram in the Notes tab.

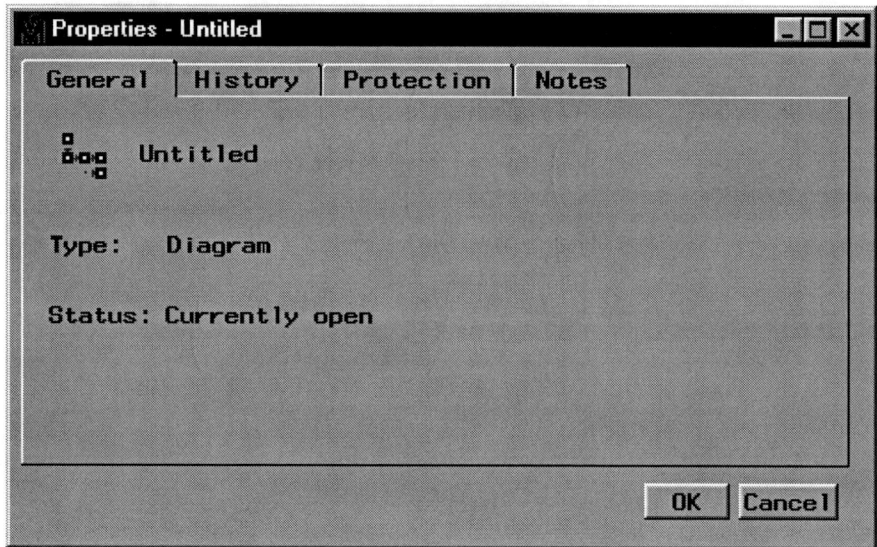

□ **Actions**

   □ **Open** — opens the selected node.

   □ **Run** — runs the selected node and any predecessor nodes in the process flow that have not been previously executed.

   □ **Results** — opens the results browser for those nodes that generate results.

   □ **Add Node** — opens the Add node window that enables you to add a new node to the Diagram Workspace.

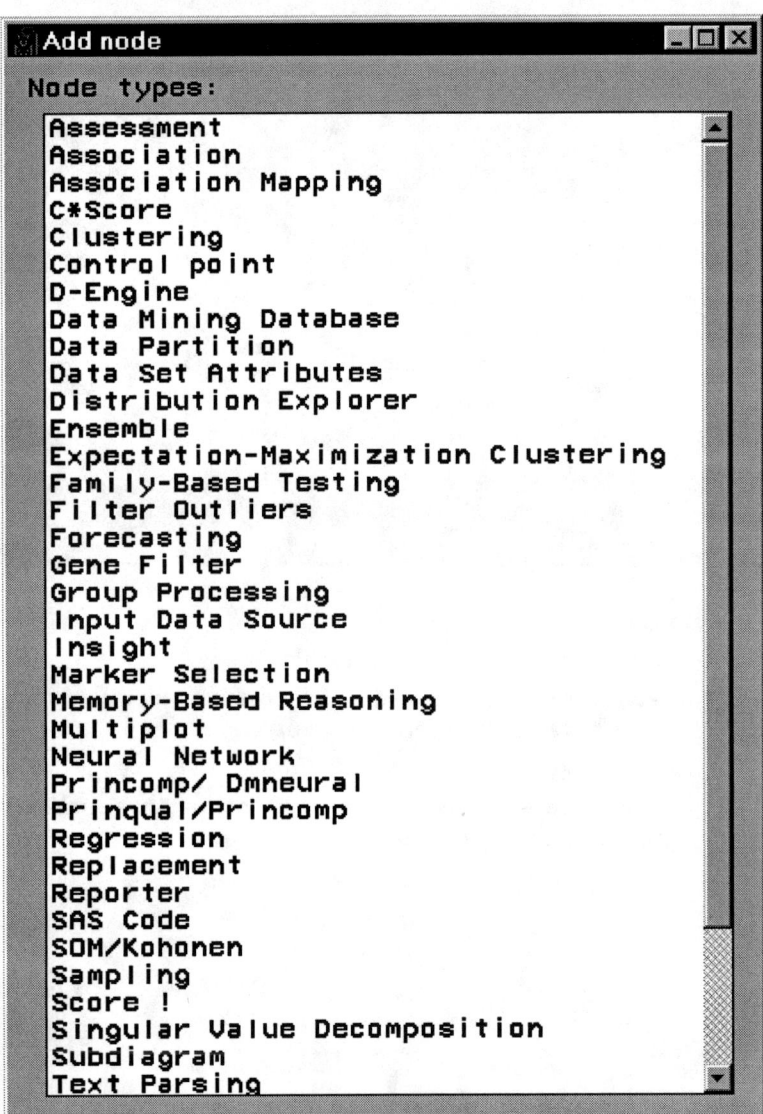

□ **Add Endpoints** — add endpoints to the process flow.

□ **Help**

  □ **Getting Started with Enterprise Miner** — this document in online Help format.

  □ **About Enterprise Miner** — Production release information about your copy of Enterprise Miner.

  □ **Help** — Enterprise Miner Reference Help. This is a hierarchical help listing. Window frame-based help is also available using the "What's This?" tool icon from the Enterprise Miner Toolbox.

Using the Toolbox

With Enterprise Miner, the toolbox at the top of the SAS window appears as follows:

Tool tips are displayed when you hold your mouse pointer over a tool icon. The icons of the Toolbox represent the following:

1 *Open* — opens a diagram within a project. You can also perform this task by using the main menu:

2 *Save diagram* — saves the current diagram. You can also perform this task by using the main menu

3 *Delete Current Project* — deletes the current project. You can also perform this task by using the main menu:

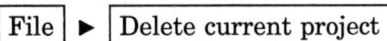

4 *User Preferences* — opens the User Preferences window that you use to specify start-up options, set the default directories for new projects, set up server profiles for client/server projects, and specify the HTML report items that you want to display when you run the *Reporter* node. You can also open the User Preferences window from the main menu:

5 *Print diagram* — prints the current process flow diagram. You can also perform this task by using the main menu:

6 *Copy diagram to clipboard* — copies the diagram to the clipboard. You can also perform this task by using the main menu:

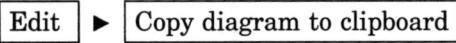

7 *What's This?* — turns the mouse pointer into a question mark, indicating that Enterprise Miner is in help mode. Click inside an Enterprise Miner window with the question mark mouse pointer to launch frame help. The window-based frame help provides information on objects in the window frame that was selected with the question mark mouse pointer.

8 *Getting Started* — launches the electronic version of this document from within Enterprise Miner.

Using the Pop-up Menus

Many of the functions found in the Enterprise Miner application main menus can be duplicated using pop-up menus. Pop-up menus are launched by right-clicking on a GUI object within Enterprise Miner. You can use pop-up menus to perform the same tasks. This documentation frequently shows you how to perform tasks using the main menu, but many of these tasks can also be performed by using the pop-up menus.

For example, instead of using the main menu to insert a diagram, follow these steps:

1 Select the Diagram tab of the Project Navigator and right-click on either the Project folder, the diagram icon, or anywhere in the background of the tab. A pop-up menu appears.

2 Select the **New Diagram** pop-up menu item. A new diagram is automatically added to the project.

Unavailable and Dimmed Items

At times particular window objects and menu items are unavailable for use. When a window object or menu item is unavailable for use, it will appear dimmed and will not respond to mouse clicks. Some window objects are grayed dynamically; that is, when an object's use is contextually inappropriate for the current data mining settings, it appears dimmed. When the data mining settings are changed so that the object's use is contextually appropriate, then the objects become active and will accept user input.

For statistical functions, dimmed objects are used to prevent the selection of inappropriate combinations of options. In some cases, specifying particular options implies that additional options must also be selected to completely specify the method or technique. Be aware that not fully specifying options can cause errors.

Enterprise Miner Documentation

In addition to this document, Enterprise Miner contains the following documentation:

☐ *Enterprise Miner Reference* — describes the usage of each Enterprise Miner node. It also contains other chapters that describe how to use various features of Enterprise Miner, such as the Target Profiler. The Enterprise Miner Reference Help is available through the application's main menu:

| Help | ▶ | EM Reference |

Note: Users can search for text strings in the EM Reference Help, using the menu choices:

| Edit | ▶ | Find |

and typing in the desired search string. △

☐ *Frame Help* — Enterprise Miner nodes have Help available at the window frame level. For Help on a field or object contained in a particular window frame:

1 Click on the **What's This?** tool icon in the Enterprise Miner Toolbox. The mouse pointer will change into a question mark.

?

2 Click inside the window that you would like help on.

3 The Enterprise Miner Help system will deliver Help on the contents of the window frame you selected.

□ *Enterprise Miner add-ins to SAS/Warehouse Administrator* — This document describes how to use the Enterprise Miner add-ins to SAS/Warehouse Administrator. To download this document in HTML format, go to the SAS web site `http://www.sas.com/software/data_warehouse`, and select the `Demos/ Downloads` link.

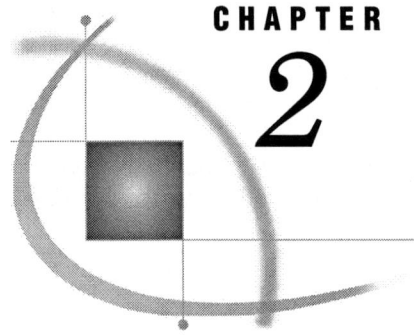

CHAPTER

2

Working with Projects

Project Overview

A project is a collection of Enterprise Miner process flow diagrams and information that pertains to them. Projects are often differentiated by the type of data that you intend to analyze. In other words, it is a good idea to create a separate project for each major data mining problem that you intend to investigate. Local projects are useful when the data is available locally on your machine. If you need to access databases on a remote host or distribute the data-intensive processing to a more powerful remote host, then you should create a client/server project.

Both local projects and client/server projects are *shareable*; that is, multiple users can work on the same project simultaneously. In order for the project to be shareable, all parties must access the same client files. The server.cfg client file uses the remote server path to point to the server, allowing multiple users to work on the same project on both the client and server side.

Although projects are shareable, only one user can open a diagram at a time. Users can create, edit, and delete diagrams without impacting the work of others sharing that project, because each diagram is an independent unit. Node clones and target profiles created by one user may be shared by other users for use in their own diagrams.

Updates to the project start-up or exit code, warehouse path, or server profile can be made only when there is one and only one person using the project. To learn about how to update these project settings, read "Viewing and Specifying Project Properties" on page 15. In a shared environment, it may be necessary to request everyone to close that project from within their own Enterprise Miner sessions, while an administrator makes the required changes. The same applies to renaming or deleting a project.

In an Enterprise Miner client/server project, the server profile is stored with the project, and as thus shared by all users of that project. This facilitates profile maintenance in a shared project environment.

Project Directory Structure

For each project, Enterprise Miner dynamically creates a number of subdirectories that have the following structure:

Note: To view your project files in a Windows file browser, select the Diagrams tab of the Enterprise Miner Project Navigator and right-click on a named project icon, then select **Explore**. △

When you create a project, Enterprise Miner automatically assigns the EMDATA and EMPROJ librefs to the EMDATA and EMPROJ subdirectories, respectively. By using a predefined directory structure and storing all of the project files in the project location (the root project directory), creating a new local project is simply a matter of supplying a project name and location. Because each project is self-contained, you can use an external application such as Windows Explorer to copy a project to another location. Enterprise Miner does not place a restriction on the number of projects. There is a limit of 100,000 diagrams per project.

Project Location

The project location directory contains the .dmp file that corresponds to the project definition, and the various .dmd files which represent the various diagrams created within the project. The name of the .dmp file defines the name of the project.

The following display shows the directory layout for a project named **Phoenix**.

This project contains a diagram named **My diagram.dmd**.

EMDATA Directory

The EMDATA directory contains potentially large files that are created when you run the process flows in your project. When running a project in client/server mode, files are written to the server data directory instead. However, samples taken from the remote location are stored in your EMDATA directory so you can continue to work when a connection to the server is unavailable.

EMPROJ Directory

Project files containing information for each diagram and its nodes, the target profiler, and various registries are stored in the EMPROJ directory. Diagram lock (.lck) files are also placed in the EMPROJ directory every time a diagram is opened. This prevents two users from opening the same diagram at the same time. The name of the lock file is always identical to the name of the diagram in question, except for the .lck extension. For example, a diagram file named **My diagram.dmd** has a corresponding **My diagram.lck** lock file.

The USERS subdirectory contains files that represent the users currently sharing the project.

REPORTS Directory

HTML reports generated by the *Reporter* node are stored in this directory. Each report has its own subdirectory. The name of the subdirectory defines the name of the report.

Viewing and Specifying Project Properties

To view and customize properties for a project, use the main menu to select

| Options | ▶ | Project | ▶ | Properties |

The Properties window opens. The properties window contains five tabs:

☐ General — displays the project name, type, share status, and location.

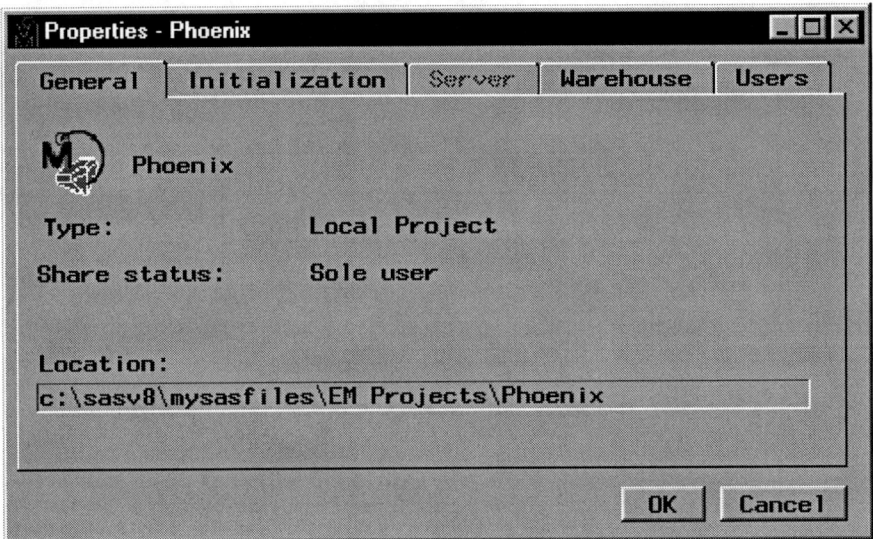

□ Initialization — specifies whether to run start-up code (such as, assigning librefs to data sources for the project or specifying the format search paths via the FMTSEARCH option) when the project is opened, and exit code (such as clearing libref assignments and resetting global SAS options) when the project is closed.

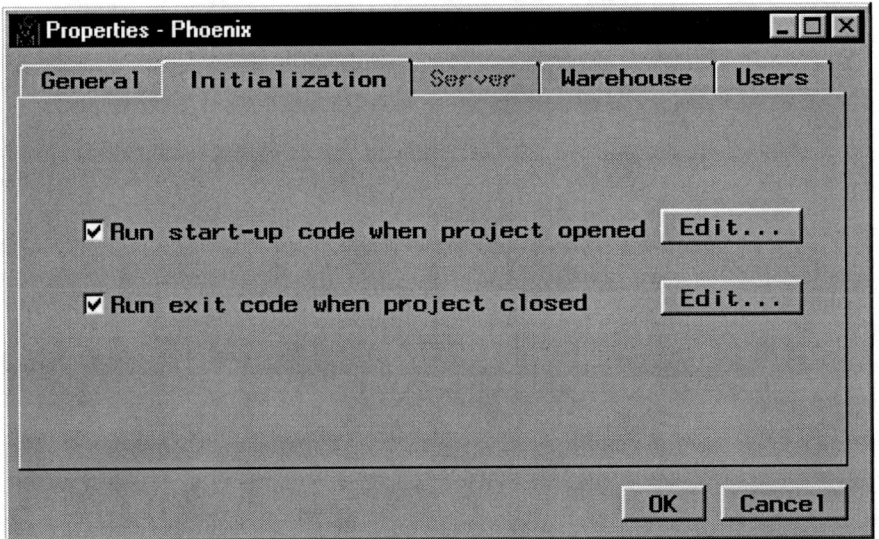

By default, start-up and exit code are enabled. To prevent either the start-up or exit code from running, deselect the appropriate check box. These options appear dimmed if the project is currently shared.

To define start-up or exit code, select the respective Edit button and type the code in the editor.

After entering your start up code, close the window and answer the prompts to save your changes.

□ Server — enables you to view and configure a default server profile. A server profile contains all the configuration information necessary to establish a connection on a remote server. You may edit the project server profile only when no one else is using the project. To learn more about this task, read "Creating a Client/Server Project" on page 20. Note that the Server tab is dimmed unless you are viewing the properties for a client/server project.

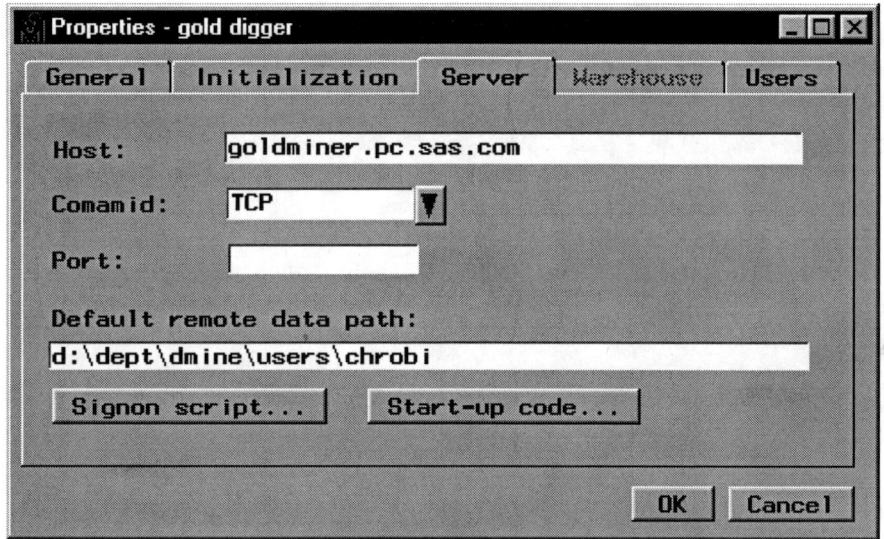

□ Warehouse — enables you to type the warehouse path where the metadata sample was created from the Enterprise Miner Addins to the SAS/Warehouse Administrator. Alternatively, you can use the Browse button to find and set the warehouse path via an explorer interface.

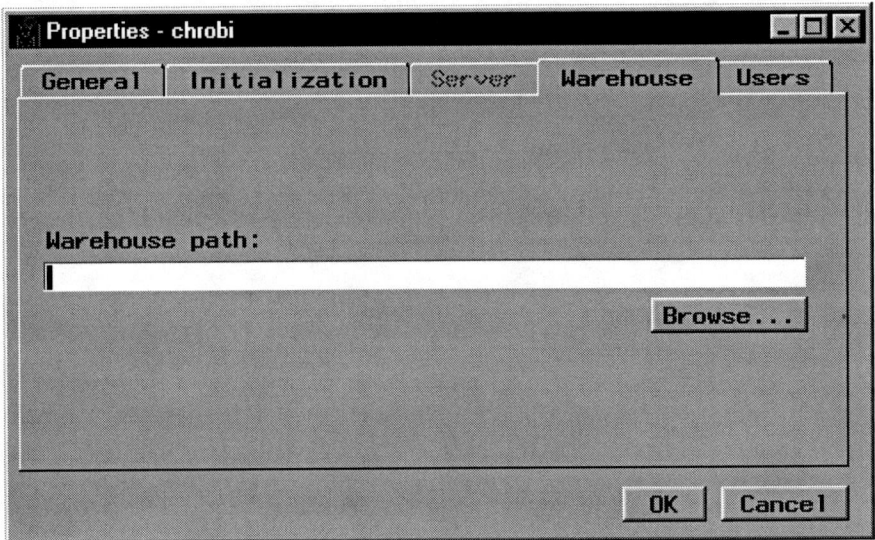

□ Users — lists the userid and sign-on time for all of the users that currently have the project open.

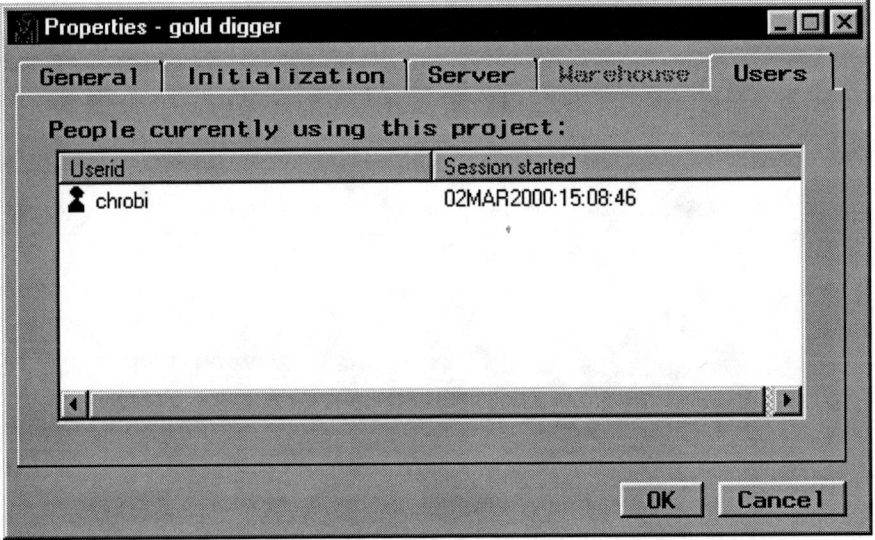

Once you have set the project properties, select the [OK] button in the Properties window or select [Cancel] to cancel your settings.

Creating a New Local Project

To create a new local project:

1 Use the **File** pull-down menu to select

The Create New Project window opens:

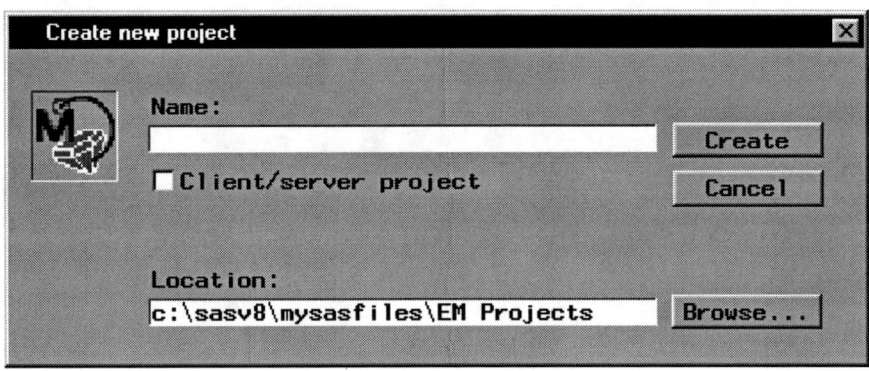

Note: To reset the default directory for new projects, use the **Options** pull-down menu to select the **User preferences** menu item. Select the Directory tab of the User preferences window and specify the default directory path for new projects. △

2 Type the location where you want the project to be stored in the **Location** field. You can also select the Browse button to browse through the folders on your machine and set the project **Location** via an explorer interface.

3 Type the project name in the **Name** entry field.

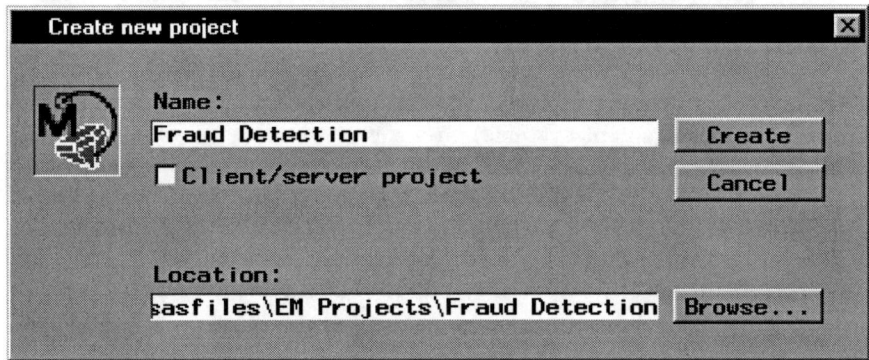

4 To create the project, select the OK button. Enterprise Miner creates the project directories, and then loads the project as the active project in the SAS Enterprise Miner window. The project contains a default diagram named Untitled.

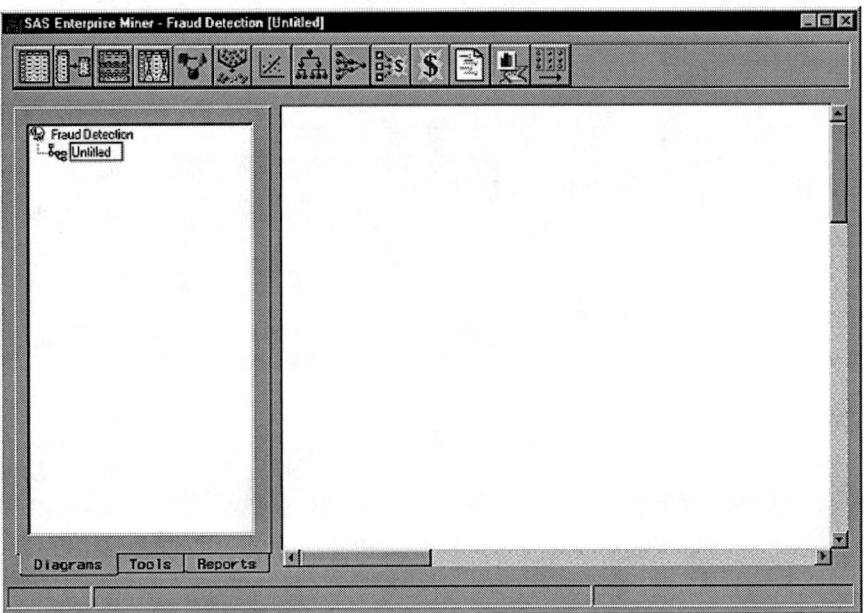

Creating a Client/Server Project

Enterprise Miner enables you to access data sources (such as SAS data sets or database management systems) on a server to use with your local SAS Enterprise Miner session. SAS/CONNECT is the cooperative processing software that establishes the client/server connection between the remote and local hosts. For complete information about SAS/CONNECT, see *SAS/CONNECT Software: Usage and Reference, Version 6, Second Edition.*

The client/server functionality provides the following advantages:

□ distributes data-intensive processing to the most appropriate machine

□ minimizes network traffic by processing the data on the server machine

□ minimizes data redundancy by maintaining one central data source

□ allows you to toggle between remote and local processing.

Defining a client/server project consists of two basic steps, which are provided via a project wizard:

1 Define the client location for the project by providing the name and a location for the project.

2 Provide a server profile. You can specify an existing profile or create a new profile.

Note: To use data sets with user-defined formats on the server, you must have the formats available locally and on the server. You can assign a format search path in a project's startup code, and in the server seed code, point to the format catalogs which exist on the client and server. △

These steps are discussed in more detail in the remainder of this section.

Defining a New Server Profile

Before you define the location and name for the client/server project, you may want to define a new server profile as part of your user preferences. A server profile contains all of the information that is necessary to establish a connection to the remote server.

To define a new server profile, follow these steps:

1 Use the **Options** pull-down menu from the SAS Enterprise Miner window to select the **User Preferences** item.

   The User Preferences window opens. You define the server profile in the Server profiles tab. This tab lists the current server profile directory and all of the profiles that are stored in this directory. By default, server profiles are stored in the SASUSER folder where Enterprise Miner was installed. To set the profile directory, select the [Browse] button to find and set the desired directory.

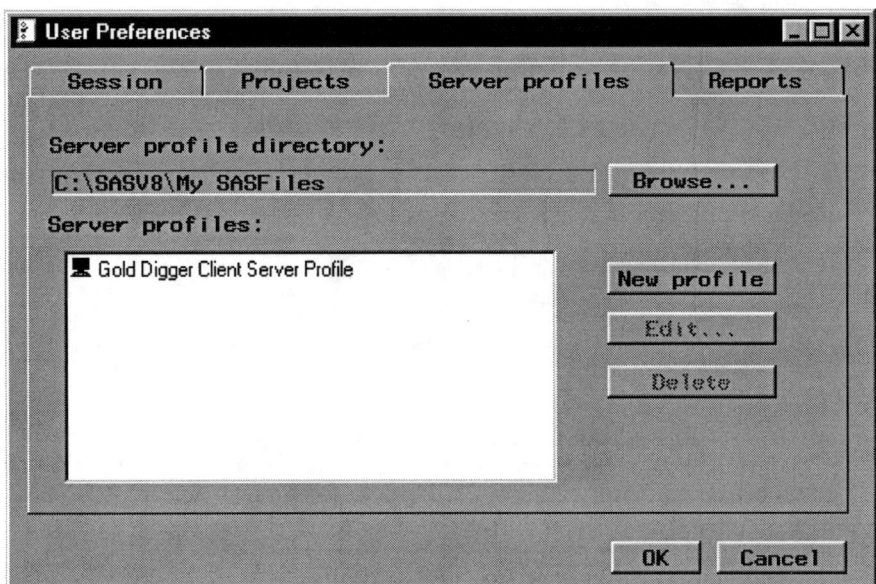

2 To create a new profile, select the [New profile] button. A new profile entry named Untitled is added to the list of server profiles.

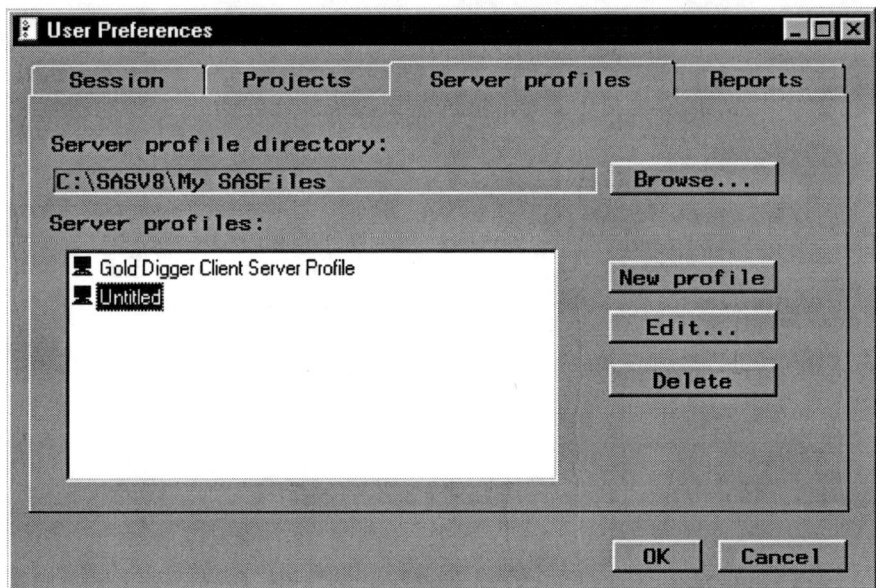

Note: To edit an existing profile, click on the $\boxed{\text{Edit}}$ button. To rename a profile, right-click on the server profile in the list and select **Rename**. Type the desired profile name. To delete a profile, use the $\boxed{\text{Delete}}$ button. △

3 Type a more descriptive profile name.

4 Click on the $\boxed{\text{Edit}}$ button. The Edit a Server Profile window opens.

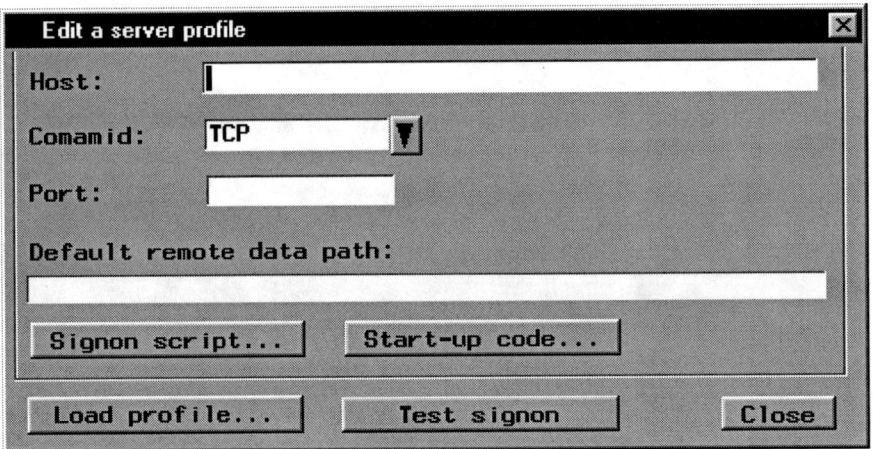

Note: To load the profile settings from an existing profile, select the $\boxed{\text{Load profile}}$ button. Select the *.srv file that contains the profile settings for the existing server. △

5 Type the remote host address name. The **Host** can be the machine name (for example, golddigger.pc.sas.com) or its numeric IP address (123.321.12.99). The address name for a NETBIOS network can contain a maximum of eight characters.

6 Select the drop-down arrow to set the **Comamid** parameter. The **Comamid** parameter identifies the communication access method that is used to connect to the remote host.

7 If a spawner is necessary to establish the remote connection, then type the Share port that the agent spawner runs on. You can type either the service name (for example , shr3) or the port number (for example, 5012). The **Port** field is required if you are running a Windows NT server where the agent spawner has been set up to run on the share port. It is not required on other platforms.

8 Type the **Default remote data path** where Enterprise Miner will store large intermediate files on the server. The path should be specified according to the host machine's naming convention. The server must be able to reference this location, and you must have write access to this path. Files in this path are accessed via remote library services when needed; they are not moved to the client.

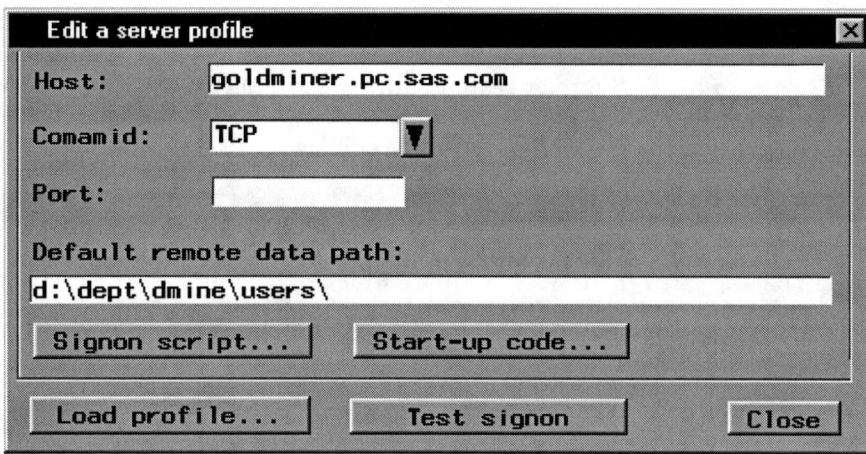

9 Set the signon script file. If **Comamid** is set to TCP, then you must set the script file that is used to initiate and terminate the remote session. A script file is an external file on the local system that contains special SAS statements that control the connection. To set the script file, follow these steps:

  a Select the Signon script button. The Signon Script window opens. At this stage, you can open an existing script, or create a new one.

  b To open an existing script, use the main menu commands:

  Alternatively, you can select the Open tool icon (third tool icon on the toolbox). Find and select the script (.scr) file in the Open window and then click the Open button. The script file is copied to the Signon Script window.

  c To create a new script file, type the script file statements in the Signon Script window or modify an existing script file to suit your needs. Save the script file by using the **File** pull-down menu to select the **Save As** menu item.

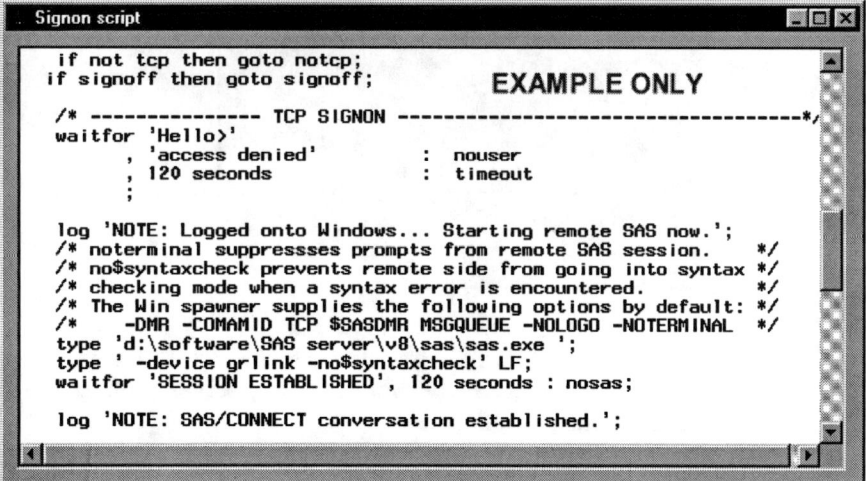

  d After you have set the script file, close the Signon Script window to return to the Edit a Server Profile window.

10 If you need to enter start-up code that runs when the server is initialized, select the Start-up Code button. The Start-up Code window opens. Type the start-up code in the Start-up Code window. You do not need to enclose the statements in an

rsubmit; endsubmit; block. You might want to use this feature to assign a libref to a remote directory that contains SAS data sets via a LIBNAME statement or assign the SAS format search path via the FMTSEARCH option. When you have finished entering your start-up code, close the window. Your code is saved and you return to the Edit a Server Profile window.

11 To test the server profile, select the ⌐Test signon⌐ button.

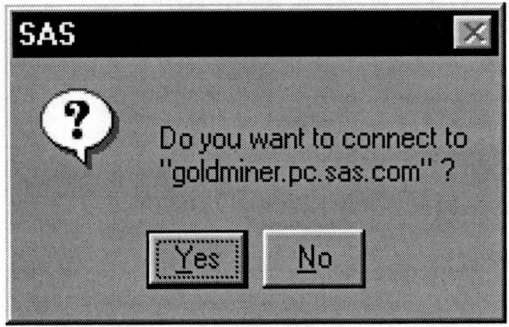

The Test Result window opens indicating whether or not Enterprise Miner was able to establish a connection to the server.

If the connection failed, cycle back through the above steps to determine where you may have incorrectly configured the server profile. You may want to consult your systems administrator.

Once you have configured the server profile, close the Edit a Server Profile window. A message window opens that prompts you to save your changes to the server profile. Select ⌐Yes⌐ to save your changes. Select ⌐No⌐ to prevent your changes from being saved and to return to the SAS Enterprise Miner window. Select ⌐Cancel⌐ to return to the Edit a Server Profile window.

How to Create a Client/Server Project

To create a client/server project, follow these steps:

1 Use the main menu to select

The Create New Project window opens:

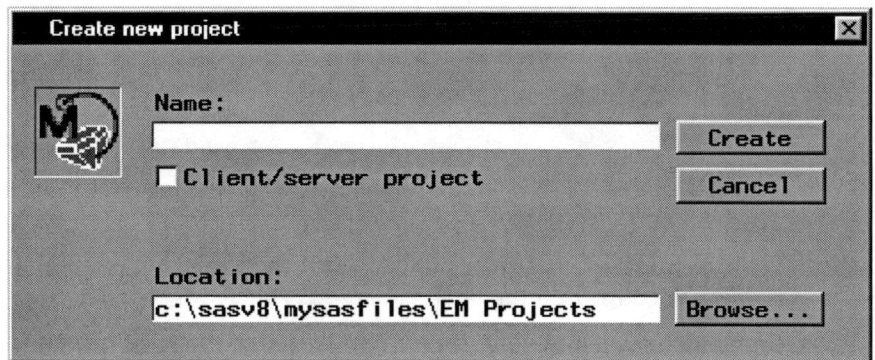

2 Set the client **Location** for the project and the **Name** and then click the **Client/ server project** check box. To set the location, type the path in the **Location** field.

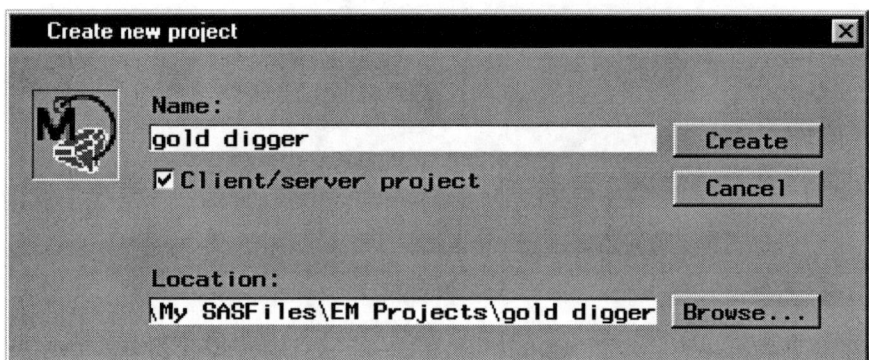

3 Select the ⌐Create⌐ button in the Create New Project window. The Client/server project window opens:

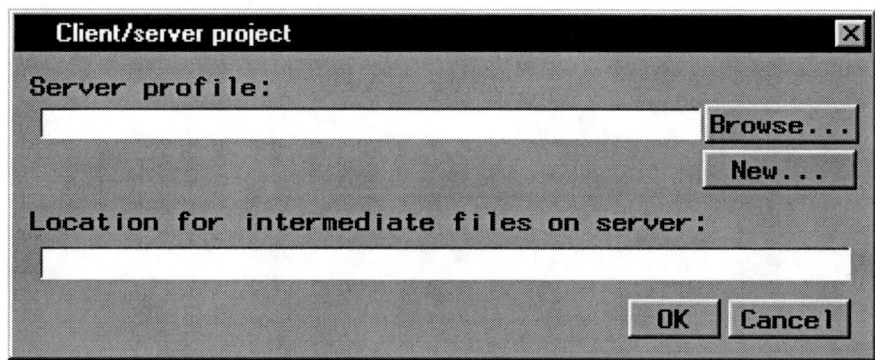

4 Specify an existing **Server profile** or create a new one.

☐ To specify an existing server profile (a .srv file), use the Browse button to find and set the server profile or type the server profile path name. You can also define a server profile in advance as part of the user preferences.

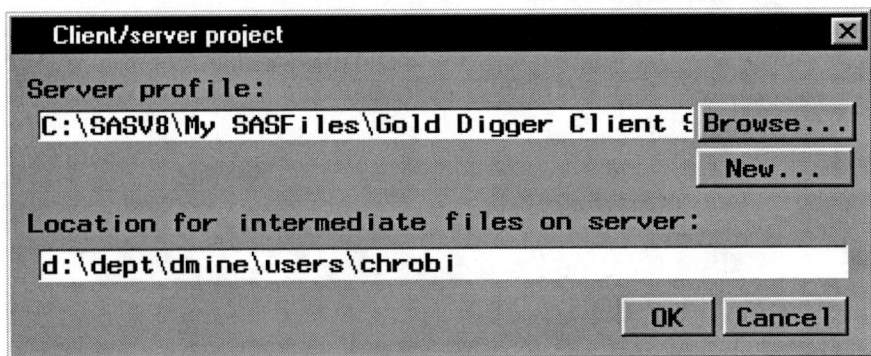

☐ To create a new server profile, select the New button. Follow the steps outlined in "Defining a New Server Profile" on page 20.

5 Once you have defined the server profile, select the OK button to create the client/server project.

6 A message window opens asking you if you want to connect to the server.

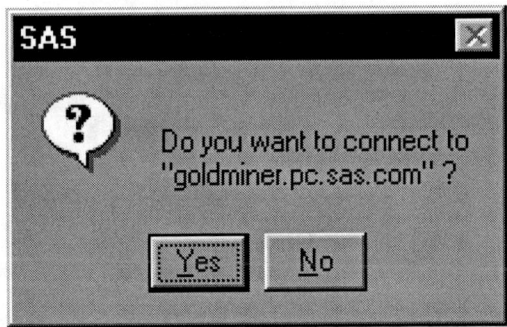

Select Yes to connect to the server or select No to run the project locally. The project is automatically loaded as the active project in the SAS Enterprise Miner window. The connection status indicator at the lower-right corner of the window indicates whether or not the project is connected to the server.

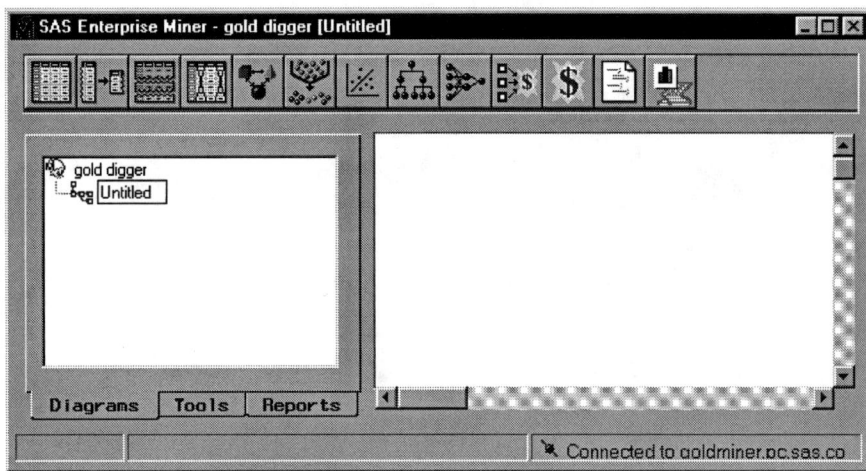

To disconnect from the server, right-click on the project folder in the Project Navigator and select the **Disconnect from server** pop-up menu item.

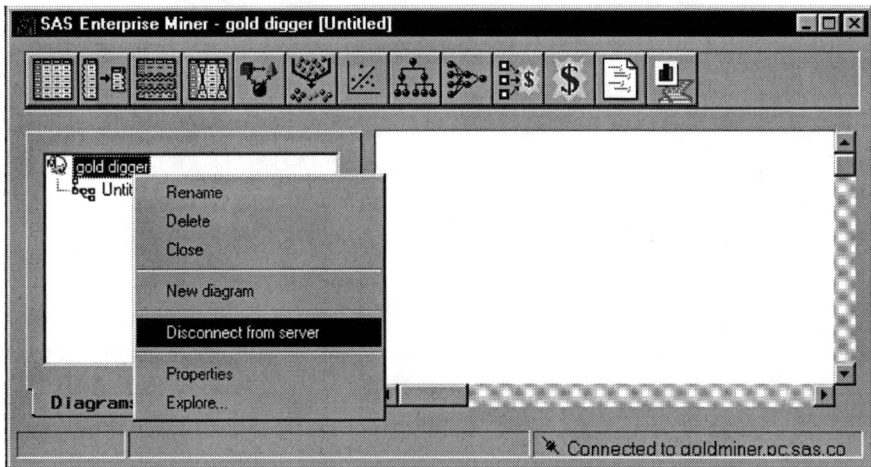

To connect to the server, right-click on the project folder in the Project Navigator and select the **Connect to server** pop-up menu item.

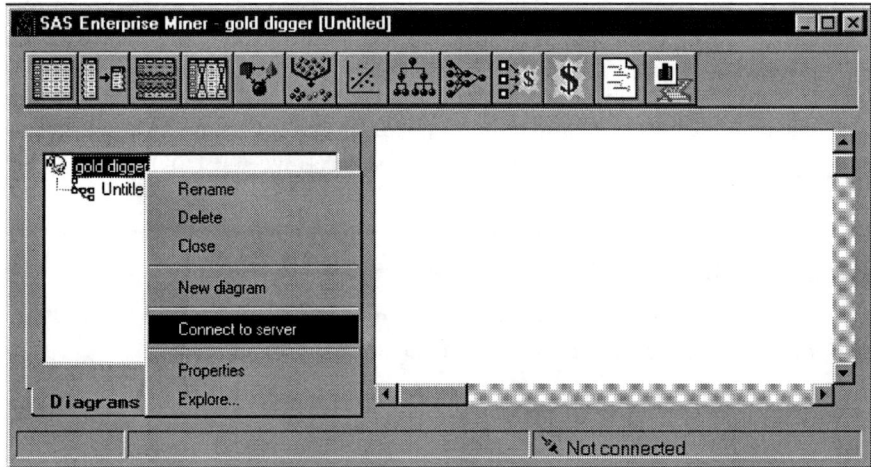

Select the Yes button in the confirmation prompt window

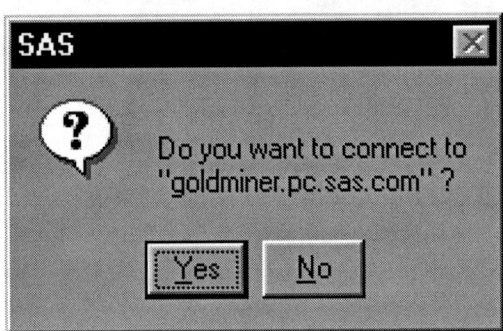

Note: You can also double-click on the connection status indicator to connect to the server. △

If you have an application that launches Enterprise Miner, but establishes a connection beforehand, you can ensure that Enterprise Miner uses the existing connection by editing the server.cfg file in your project's EMPROJ subdirectory.

Type the **CONID** for the existing connection. For example, if your application connects to a server using CONID=myhost, then you would type this value for the CONID option in your server.cfg file. When you make these changes Enterprise Miner will not try to make a connection when opening the project if a connection already exists. Likewise, when Enterprise Miner is instructed not to make an connection when opening a project, Enterprise Miner will also not terminate the connection when the project is closed.

Using a Server Profile in Batch Mode to Connect to a Server

You can use your server profile in batch mode to connect to the server by submitting the following code from the Program Editor window of SAS:

```
%let profile=c:\profiles\my server.srv;
proc display c=sashelp.dmcon.connect.scl;
run;
```

Note: The code assumes that your server profile is named 'my server.srv' and is stored in c:\profiles. You should modify those parameters to match the server profile name and storage path with the ones on your intstallation. △

Opening a Process Flow Diagram

To open a process flow diagram within the project:

1 Select the Diagrams tab of the Project Navigator if it is not already active.

2 Double-click on the diagram icon or label that you want to open. Alternatively, you can right-click on the diagram label and select the **Open** pop-up menu item.

When a selected diagram is opened, the Diagram Workspace becomes active, and the diagram can be edited, run, and saved. A diagram contains the data mining process flow that you build interactively. You can think of a diagram as a type of graphical computer program. To learn more about building process flow diagrams, read "Components Used to Build Process Flow Diagrams" on page 37.

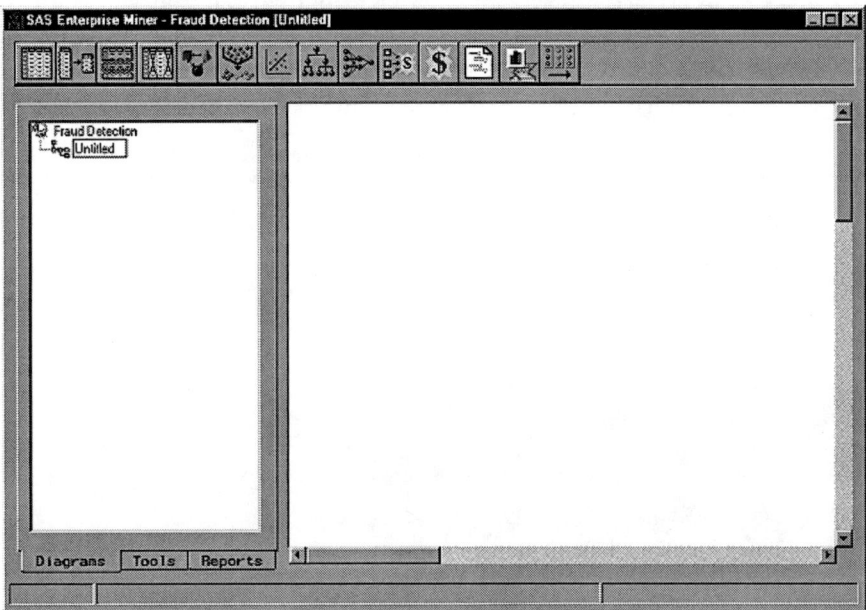

Note: The fraud detection project contains one diagram named Untitled. You can have more than one diagram for each project. △

Opening an Existing Project

To open an existing project or a diagram within that project, follow these steps:

1 Use the main menu to select

File ▶ Open

or you can just click the Open tool icon in the toolbox.

In the Open window, browse through the folders on your machine to find the project .dmp file or the diagram .dmd file.

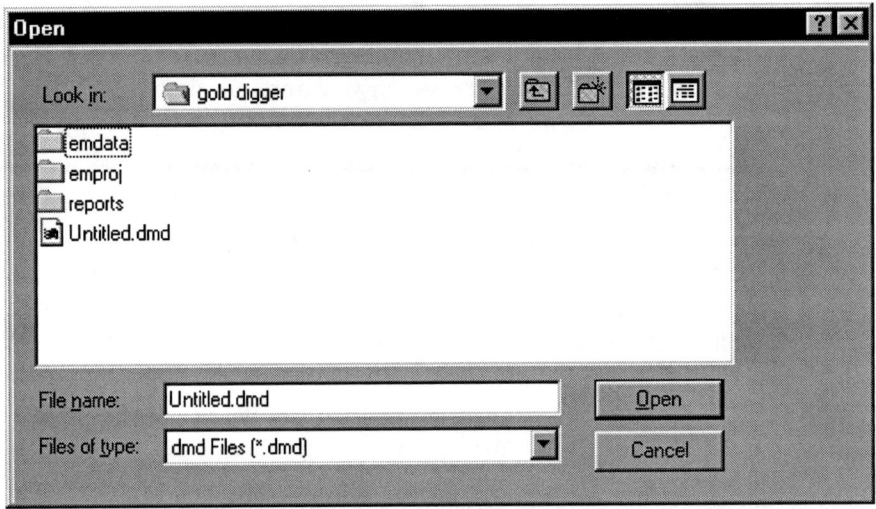

2 Select the project .dmp file or the diagram .dmd file that you want to open. If you select a diagram .dmd file that is already opened by another user, then a message window appears indicating that the diagram is locked.

Select the OK button to open the project.

Once you have opened a project, you must work with an existing diagram in the project, create a new diagram, or wait until a locked diagram becomes available.

Note: Multiple users can open the same project (.dmp file) but not the same diagram (.dmd file) within the project. △

Note: If the project is a client/server project, then a message window appears asking if want to connect to the server.

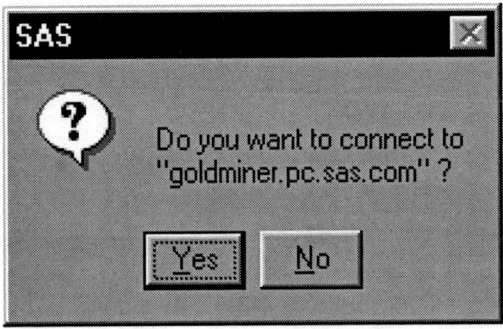

Select Yes to establish a connection to the server or select No to run the project locally. △

Saving a Project Diagram

To save a project diagram, first close any open nodes in the Diagram Workspace. Then, use the **File** pull-down menu to select the **Save diagram** menu item.

Note that you can also perform this function by selecting the Save Diagram tool icon on the Tools Bar.

To save the current diagram to a different name, use the **File** menu to select the **Save diagram as** menu item. The Save Diagram As window opens. Type the diagram name in the **Save as** field and then select the OK button.

Running a Project Diagram

To generate results from a process flow diagram, you must run the process flow path to execute the code that is associated with each node. The paths can be run in several ways:

- ☐ When the node in the Diagram Workspace is closed and selected (a dotted line surrounds selected nodes), you can use the main menu:

    Actions ▶ Run

- ☐ Also if the node in the Diagram Workspace is closed, you can

    1 Right-click the node to open a pop-up menu.

    2 Select the **Run** pop-up menu item.

- ☐ Many nodes, including all of the modeling nodes, can be run when the nodes' tabbed configuration window is open. To run an open modeling node, select the **Run** icon on the toolbox or use the main menu:

    Tools ▶ Train Model

    For non-modelling nodes, the main menu selection is

    Tools ▶ Run <Node Name>

    You must run the predecessor nodes in your process flow diagram before you can run an open node.

When a node in a process flow diagram is run, a green box surrounds each node icon in succession as information is passed from node to node in the process flow. When you run a process flow diagram that contains a *Group Processing* node, a blue box surrounds the *Group Processing* node icon to indicate the beginning of each loop iteration. If the process flow diagram contains a *Reporter* node, yellow boxes surround the predecessor nodes to indicate that the HTML reports are being generated. Red boxes surround nodes that fail when executed. To determine the error condition associated with a failed node, use the main menu

View ▶ Messages

In most cases, if you have *not* run the predecessor nodes in the process flow, then these nodes automatically run when you run the selected successor node. If you *have* already run the predecessor nodes in the process flow, and you have not changed any of the node settings in the interim, then they do not run when you run the selected successor node. Any nodes that follow the selected node are *not* run.

When the path has executed, a message dialog box opens stating that the task is completed.

Select the OK button to close the message dialog box.

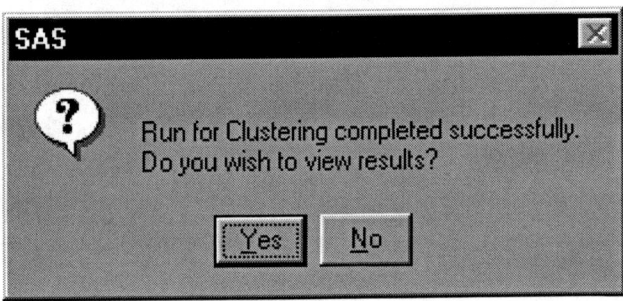

Note: The message dialog box for any node with results asks you if you want to view the results. Select the [Yes] button to view the results in a result browser. Select the [No] button if you do not want to view the results. △

You can view the results for nodes that generate results by right–clicking on the node icon and selecting the **Results** pop-up menu item. Alternatively, use the main menu:

 [Actions] ▶ [Results]

Closing Projects and Diagrams

To close a project that is open, right-click the project folder in the Project Navigator and select the **Close** pop-up menu item. You can also use the main menu:

[File] ▶ [Close project]

Both methods automatically save your changes to the project.
To close a diagram, use the main menu:

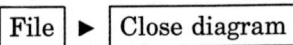 [File] ▶ [Close diagram]

Creating a New Diagram

To create a new diagram, follow these steps:
1 Open the project which will contain the new diagram.
2 Right-click anywhere in the Diagram tab of the Project Navigator and select the **New Diagram** pop-up menu item.
3 By default, a new diagram named Untitled is added to the project. An *n* subscript is added to the diagram name to distinguish untitled diagrams.

Alternatively, you can use the main menu:

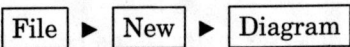 [File] ▶ [New] ▶ [Diagram]

The diagram becomes active in the Diagram Workspace. To rename the diagram, right-click on the diagram label in the Project Navigator and select the **Rename** pop-up menu item.

Deleting Projects and Diagrams

To delete a project, first open the project to be deleted, then right-click on the project name in the Project Navigator and choose **Delete current project.**

Alternately, you could select the project name in the Project Navigator and use the main menu:

| File | ▶ | Delete current project |

A dialog box prompts you to verify the deletion.

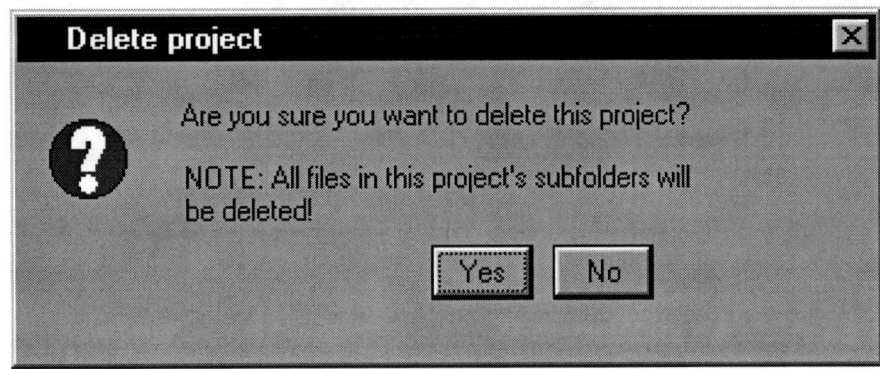

Select the Yes button to verify that the project is to be deleted, or select the No button to cancel the deletion.

CAUTION:

If you placed your own files within the project's directory tree structure (for example, a SAS data set), then these files are also deleted when you delete the project. *All files within the project folder are deleted!* △

Other ways to delete a project include the following:

□ Delete the root project directory from outside of Enterprise Miner using another tool, such as Windows Explorer. In order to delete it from outside of Enterprise Miner, the project must not be open. You can only delete local projects with this method.

You can only delete a project if you are the sole user.

If you delete a client/server project when you are connected to the server, then all of the project files are deleted — including those on the remote host. If you are not connected to the server, and choose not to reconnect, then only the local project files are deleted. A local "kill" file named "*projectname*_kill.sas" is written to the project root directory. When you submit this kill file from the SAS Program Editor window, a connection is established to the server and then the project remote files are deleted.

To delete a diagram, right-click on the diagram name in the Project Navigator and then select the **Delete** pop-up menu item. A dialog box prompts you to verify the deletion.

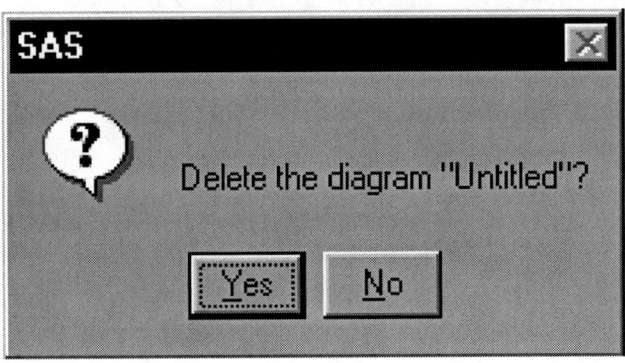

Select the Yes button to verify that the diagram is to be deleted, or select the No button to cancel the deletion.

Project Troubleshooting Tips

If Enterprise Miner inadvertently crashes or program halts, then the .lck file for the diagram usually does not get deleted. This will prevent you from reopening the diagram in a new Enterprise Miner session, because you will actually hold a lock on the diagram. If this occurs, follow these steps:

1 Close your Enterprise Miner session.

2 Use Windows Explorer or a suitable file utility to locate and open the EMPROJ subfolder for the project.

3 Find the .lck file that matches the diagram you were working on and delete it.

4 Restart Enterprise Miner and open the diagram.

If you restart Enterprise Miner and the Project Properties window indicates the project is currently being shared, but you know that you are the only person using the project, then Enterprise Miner was also probably not shutdown properly. In this case, follow these steps:

1 Close all Enterprise Miner sessions.

2 Make sure that no one else is using the project.

3 Use Windows Explorer or a suitable file utility to open the EMPROJ folder for the project.

4 Open the USERS folder and delete its contents, but not delete the USERS folder!

5 Restart Enterprise Miner and reopen the project.

If you try to open a project and are informed by a message window that the project libraries could not be assigned, then either the EMPROJ or EMDATA library are still in use. A few potential reasons why the EMPROJ or EMDATA library is still in use include the following:

□ An FSVIEW window for a data set in either library could be open

□ An CATALOG window is open

□ A data set or some other SAS file was not closed properly by Enterprise Miner.

You should first try to find and close the window that is using the data set or file. If you are still unable to open the project, you should close and then restart Enterprise Miner. If this fails as well, then close and restart SAS.

Exporting Version 4.0 Projects

In Enterprise Miner Version 4.0, the project export wizard has been removed. Since Version 3.0 and 4.0 projects are self contained in the project root directory, exporting a project simply involves copying or moving the entire project to the desired target location using an external application such as Windows Explorer. You may also want to use a third party application such as Winzip to archive the project before exporting it to a new location. You can unzip the project in your new directory.

For Version 3.0 and Version 4.0 client/server projects, you should archive the server files separately from the client files.

Importing a Version 2.0x Project

You can also import Version 2.0x DMX files with some restrictions:

□ Version 2.0x DMX files that were created from the projects located in the WORK library will be imported as temporary projects. When a temporary project is closed, it is deleted.

□ Version 2.0x DMX files that were created using SASUSER or SASHELP as either the data or project library cannot be imported.

To import a Version 2.0x project directly, follow these steps:

1 Invoke Enterprise Miner and use the **File** pull-down menu to select the **Import Version 2 project** item.

2 Set the **Old project library location** and the **New project location** in the Import Version 2 project window:

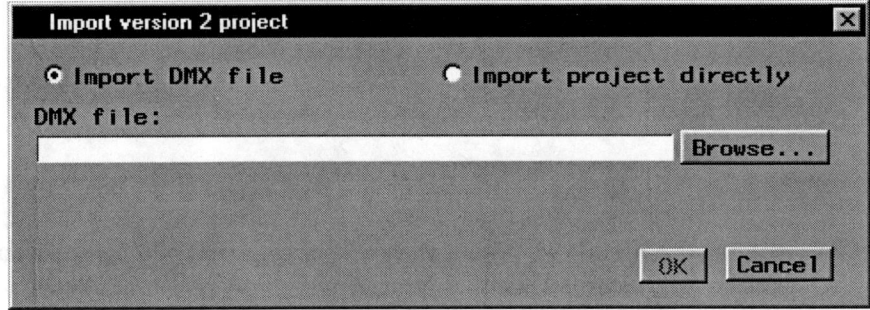

3 Select the [Browse] button to find the .dmx file to import, then click [OK]. The project is loaded as the active project.

You must not have an Enterprise Miner 2.0x session open when importing the project. You can only import 2.0x projects that are on the same PC as your Enterprise Miner 4.0 session. Enterprise Miner 2.0x projects using either SASUSER or SASHELP as the project data library cannot be imported. Enterprise Miner 2.0x WORK (temporary) projects cannot be imported using this method.

Opening a Version 3.0x Project

To open a Version 3.0x project directly, follow these steps:

1 Invoke Enterprise Miner and from the main menu, select

$\boxed{\text{File}}$ ► $\boxed{\text{Open}}$

2 Use the interface to locate the version 3.0x project directory. In the Version 3.0x project directory, select the project and click on $\boxed{\text{Open}}$.

3 A Conversion to V8 Required window opens.

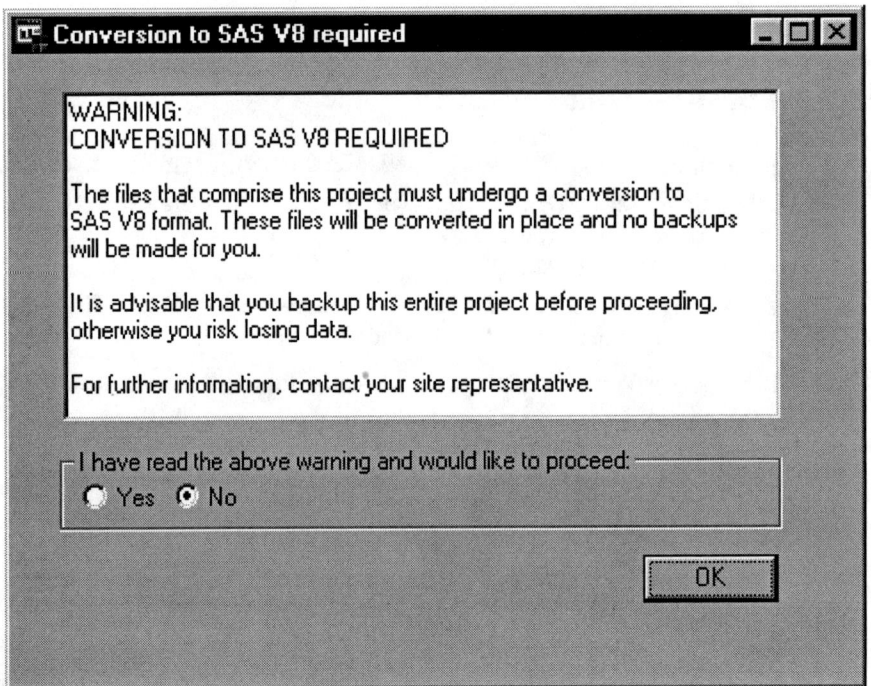

Note: We strongly recommend you back up your Version 3.0x project before opening it in Enterprise Miner 4.0. Do not revisit that project using SAS 6.12 after it has been converted. Although it will appear that you can add and delete diagrams, the project file will become corrupt. If you want to use separate versions of Enterprise Miner on the same project, you should make a copy of the project files to use with Enterprise Miner 3.0x and use a different copy for conversion and use in Enterprise Miner 4.0. △

4 Select the **Yes** radio button and $\boxed{\text{OK}}$ to proceed with the conversion.

For information on converting Version 6 data sets to Version 8 data sets, see "Converting SAS Version 6 Elements" in the SAS System Help.

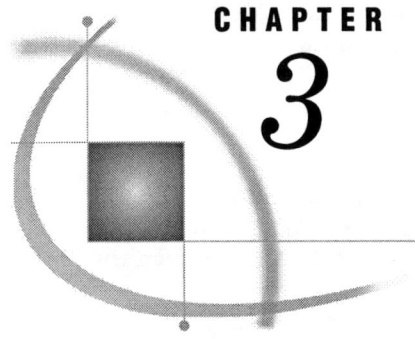

CHAPTER

3

Building Process Flow Diagrams

Components Used to Build Process Flow Diagrams

After opening a project diagram, you use the Diagram Workspace, the Tools Palette of the Project Navigator, and the Tools Bar to edit and modify the diagram; that is, you can add nodes, connect nodes, cut connections, and delete nodes.

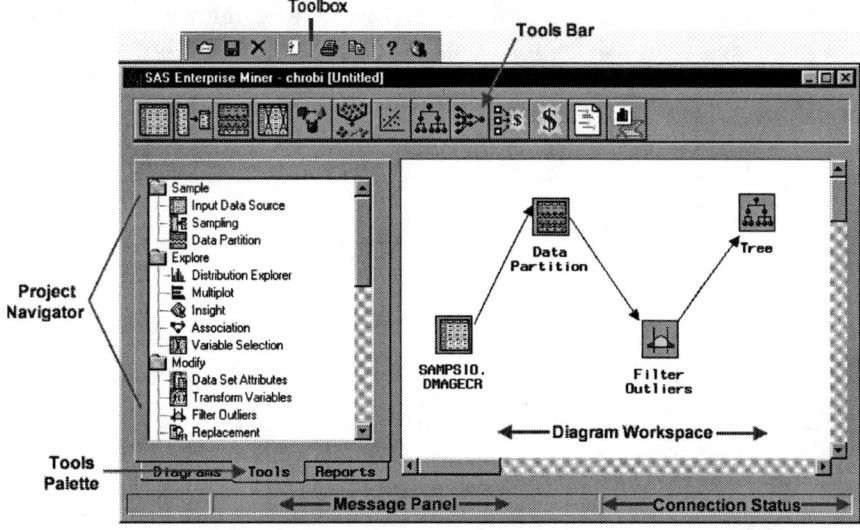

The Toolbox and the application main menus at the top of the SAS Enterprise Miner window also contain useful items for constructing process flow diagrams.

The Tools Palette

The Tools Palette in the Project Navigator displays all of the data mining tools that are available for constructing process flow diagrams. The tools are group according to the phase of the SEMMA data mining process. You drag and drop nodes from the Tools Palette onto the Diagram Workspace.

To view the properties of a node, right-click on the tool icon and select the **Properties** pop-up menu item. To learn more about this task, read "Viewing and Setting Node Defaults" on page 65.

For a description of the nodes, read "Organization of Enterprise Miner Nodes" on page 49.

The Tools Bar

By default, the Tools Bar contains a subset of Enterprise Miner tools that are commonly used to build process flow diagrams in the Diagram Workspace. You can also drag and drop tools from the Tools Bar onto the Diagram Workspace. To display tool tips, move your mouse pointer slowly over the icons on the Tools Bar (do not press down any of the mouse buttons).

To reposition a tool on the Tools Bar, drag and drop the tool icon to the desired location.

To add a node from the Tools Palette to the Tools Bar, drag and drop the tool icon from the Tools Palette to the Tools Bar.

To remove a tool from the Tools Bar, right-click on the tool icon and select **Remove from tool bar**.

To view the properties for a tool, right-click on a tool icon and select **Tool Properties**.

The Messages Window

The Messages window displays messages that are generated by the creation or execution of a process flow diagram. The Messages window is useful for detecting errors that may have occurred when running a node or a process flow path. To display the Messages window, use the **View** pull-down menu to select the **Messages** menu item. The Messages window appears on your desktop. You must close the Messages window to continue working with the process flow diagram.

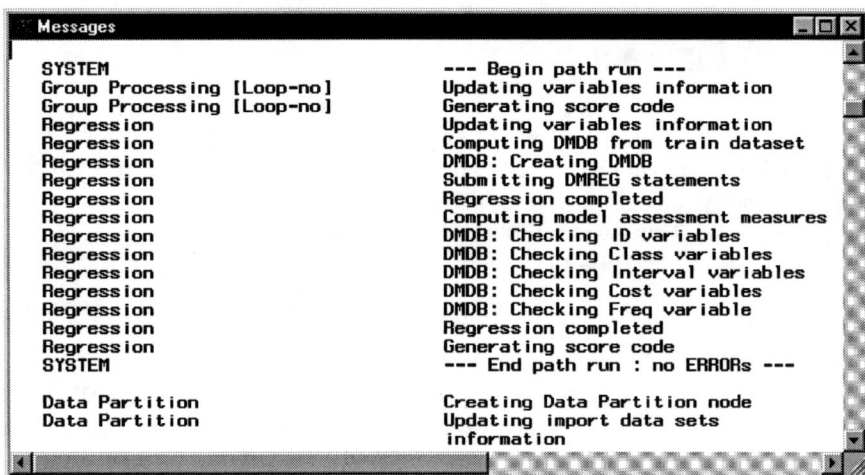

The messages are stored as part of the diagram. They may be cleared from within the Messages window by selecting from the main menu:

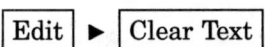

Edit ► Clear Text

Note: Messages are also displayed in the message panel when you create or execute a process flow diagram. The message panel is the second panel along the bottom of the SAS Enterprise Miner window. △

Using the Diagram Workspace Pop-up Menu

You can use the Diagram Workspace pop-up menus to perform many tasks. To open the pop-up menu, right-click in an open area of the Diagram Workspace. (Note that you can also perform many of these tasks using the pull-down menus.) The pop-up menu contains the following items:

- **Add node** — accesses the Add node window.
- **Add endpoints** — adds enter and exit endpoints to a subdiagram.
- **Paste** — pastes a node from the clipboard to the Diagram Workspace.
- **Undelete** — undeletes the last deleted node.
- **Delete** — deletes the selected node.
- **Select All** — selects all nodes in the process flow diagram.
- **Create subdiagram** — creates a subdiagram (see "Subdiagrams" on page 54). Note that to create a subdiagram, you must first select the nodes and connections that are to be included in the subdiagram.
- **Refresh** — refreshes the image that is displayed in the Enterprise Miner window.
- **Up one level** — collapses a subdiagram.
- **Top level** — moves to the top level of the process flow diagram. At the top level, all subdiagrams are condensed.
- **Connect items** — a mode of editing where node icons are fixed in location so it is easier to connect nodes.
- **Move items** — a mode of editing where node icons cannot be connected so it is easier to move nodes.
- **Move and connect** — the default mode of editing where node icons can be moved and connected.

Adding Nodes to a Diagram

You add nodes to the Diagram Workspace to create a process flow. Nodes should be connected in a logical order that represents the desired components of the sample, explore, modify, model, and assess (SEMMA) methodology. In general, the flow of your process flow diagrams should follow this methodology.

You can add nodes to a process flow diagram in five ways:

☐ Drag and drop node icons from the Tools Palette of the Project Navigator to the Diagram Workspace.

☐ Drag and drop node icons from the Tools Barto the Diagram Workspace. This task is accomplished the same way that you drag and drop nodes from the Tools Palette.

☐ Use the Diagram Workspace pop-up menu. Right-click on an open area in the Diagram Workspace, and select the **Add node** pop-up menu item. The Add node window appears.

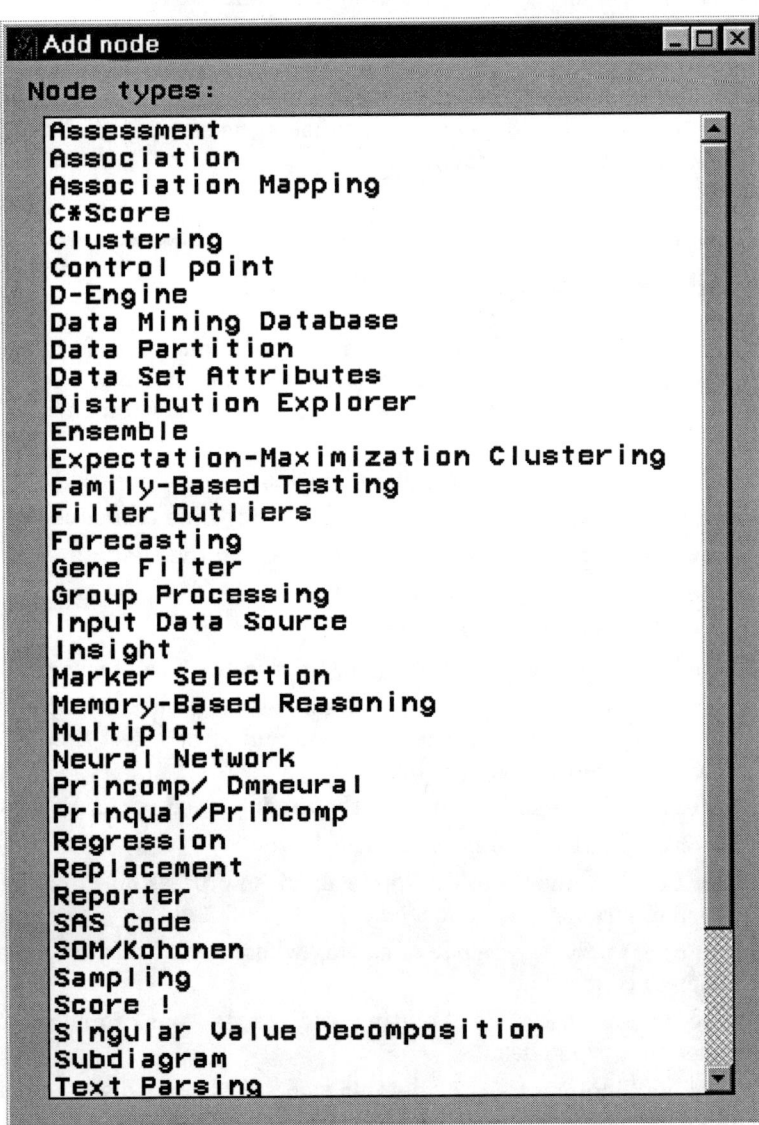

Select the desired node from the list of nodes. The node appears in the Diagram Workspace.

- □ Double-click an open area in the Diagram Workspace to display the Add Node window.

- □ Using the **Actions** pull-down menu to select the **Add Node** menu item. This action opens the Add Node window.

Using the Node Pop-up Menu

To open a node pop-up menu, right-click on a node icon in the Diagram Workspace. The node pop-up menu contains the following items:

- □ **Open** — opens the node.
- □ **Run** — runs both the selected node and all predecessor nodes in the process flow diagram that have not been run.
- □ **Results** — opens the node results browser for those nodes that generate results. You must run the node before you can open the results browser.
- □ **Copy** — copies the node to the paste buffer.

    Note: To paste the node onto the Diagram Workspace, use the **Edit** pull-down menu to select the **Paste** menu item.

- □ **Delete** — deletes the node.
- □ **Clone** — clones a node.
- □ **About** — displays node properties in the About window.
- □ **Connect items** — a mode of editing where node icons are fixed in location so it is easier to connect nodes.
- □ **Move items** — a mode of editing where node icons cannot be connected so it is easier to move nodes.
- □ **Move and connect** — the default mode of editing where node icons can be moved and connected.

Connecting Nodes in a Diagram

You connect nodes in the Diagram Workspace to create a logical process flow. When you create a process flow, you should follow the *Sample, Explore, Modify, Model,* and *Assess (SEMMA)* data mining methodology. Information flows from node to node in the direction that the connecting arrows point. There are three editing modes available in the Diagram Workspace. You can right-click on a node to access these modes:

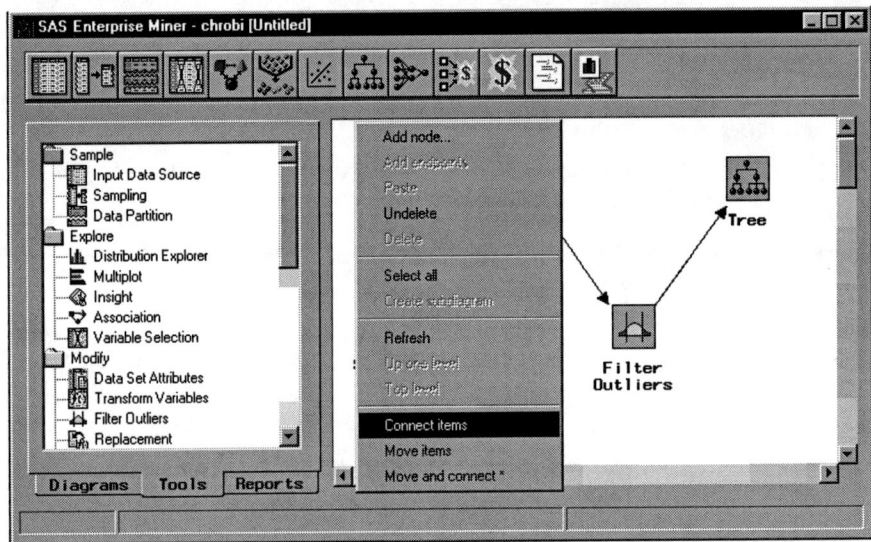

- □ **Connect Items** — Enables you to create connections between nodes. In this editing mode, the nodes are fixed in location, so that you can more easily make connections.

- □ **Move Items** — Enables you to move nodes from one location to another within the Diagram Workspace. In this editing mode, you cannot make connections.

- □ **Move and Connect** — The default mode you use to move and connect items.

As an example of connecting nodes, try to connect the *Input Data Source* node to the *Sampling* node. Assuming that the *Input Data Source* node is located to the left of the *Sampling* node, the steps to create a connection are as follows:

1 Move the mouse pointer to the right edge of the *Input Data Source* icon. The mouse pointer changes from an arrow to a cross.

2 Select and hold the left mouse button down, drag the mouse pointer to the left edge of the *Sampling* node icon, and release the mouse button. A successful connection results in a line segment that joins the two nodes.

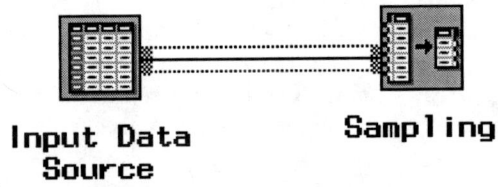

Note that if the *Input Data Source* icon moves (instead of making a connection), then you should right-click on the node icon and select the **Connect items** pop-up menu item. You can also move the mouse pointer away from the icons and single-click the left mouse button, and then attempt to make the connection.

3 Move the mouse pointer away from the node icons, and click the mouse pointer on a blank area. The line segment that connects the tool icon becomes an arrow, coming from the *Input Data Source* node icon and pointing at the *Sampling* node icon. The direction of the arrow is important because it indicates the direction of the information flow from one node to the next. In this example, the *Input Data*

Source node is the predecessor node, and the *Sampling* node is the successor node in the process flow.

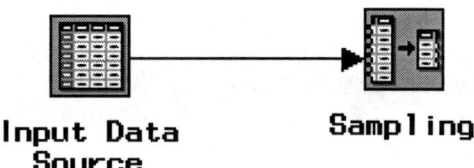

You use this same technique to connect additional nodes. Most nodes can have multiple predecessor and successor nodes. See "Usage Rules for Nodes" on page 58 for more information.

Cutting Connections in a Diagram

To cut a connection between two nodes, follow these steps:

1 Select the arrow that connects the nodes. The arrow changes to a line segment.

2 Allow the mouse pointer to remain on the line segment, and then right-click to open a pop-up menu.

3 Select the **Delete** pop-up menu item. The line segment disappears from the Diagram Workspace, and the nodes are no longer connected. Cutting the connection between node icons cuts the information flow between those nodes.

Deleting Nodes from a Diagram

To delete a node from the process flow diagram, follow these steps:

1 Right-click on the node icon to open a pop-up menu.

2 Select the **Delete** pop-up menu item. A verification window appears asking you to verify that you want to delete this node. If you select the OK button, then the node is removed from the process flow diagram. If you select the Cancel button, then the node remains in the process flow diagram.

Note: This task can also be performed by selecting the node and using the **Delete** tool icon from the toolbox. △

To restore the deleted node, right-click in an open area of the Diagram Workspace area and select the **Undelete** pop-up menu item. The node is copied to the Diagram

Workspace, but any previous connections are lost. You must redraw your node connections.

To delete multiple nodes, follow these steps:

1 Select a node icon that you want to delete, and then SHIFT-click or CTRL-click the remaining node icons that you want to delete. The selected nodes become highlighted. Alternatively, you can select multiple nodes by dragging your mouse pointer around the nodes that you want to delete. A box appears around the selected node icons. This technique is referred to as "rubber banding" nodes.

2 Allow the mouse pointer to remain on the selected icons, and then right–click to open a pop-up menu.

3 Select the **Delete** pop-up menu item. A verification window appears asking you to verify that you want to delete these nodes. If you select the OK button, then the nodes and their connections are removed from the process flow diagram. If you select the Cancel button, then the nodes remain in the process flow diagram.

To delete all nodes in the process flow:

1 From the main menu, select

Edit ▶ Select all

2 After all the nodes are selected, from the main menu choose

Edit ▶ Delete

or click the **Delete** icon in the Tool Box.

Note: You cannot restore a multiple node deletion. △

When you delete a predecessor node in a process flow diagram, the results are still available in the successor node(s). It is important to note that the results may not be reliable or accurate. For example, assume that you defined the following process flow diagram and ran the flow from the *Regression* node:

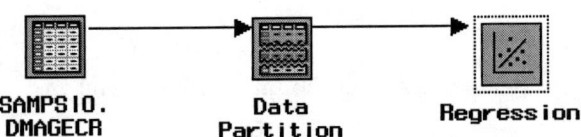

You then decide to delete the *Data Partition* node and add a new *Data Partition* node to the flow. The *Regression* node will still store the results from the first run of the flow. To obtain the updated regression results, you need to re-run the flow.

Moving Nodes in a Diagram

To move a node, follow these steps:

1 Use the mouse pointer to drag the node that you want to move. A box appears around the icon indicating that it has been selected.

2 Drag the node icon to a new position on the Diagram Workspace. Note that when you drag the node icon, the mouse pointer becomes the shape of a hand. The connection arrows will typically bend and/or stretch to accommodate the move.

Note: To move multiple nodes, first "rubber band", SHIFT-click, or CTRL-click the nodes you want to move. △

Copying and Pasting a Node

You can copy an existing node to memory and paste it in the Diagram Workspace. The same node attributes that you copy are used in the new node. You can copy a node from one diagram and paste it to another diagram if you want. However, you cannot copy a node from one project to another project. To copy an existing node, follow these steps:

1 Right-click on the node that you want to copy in the Diagram Workspace. Select the **Copy** pop-up menu item.

2 Right-click on the location where you want to paste the node. Select the **Paste** pop-up menu item.

Because a *Subdiagram* node can represent multiple nodes in a diagram, you can use this node to copy more than one node at a time.

Cloning a Node

You may want to clone a node if you plan to use the node repeatedly in a project. For example, assume that you have an input data set defined in an *Input Data Source* node. If you want to use the same input data set in the current diagram or in another diagram of the project, then you can clone the existing *Input Data Source* node. When you clone a node, it is added as a new node on the Tools Palette in the **Custom** section. When you want to use the node, you simply drag it from the Tools Palette onto the Diagram Workspace. The information that is contained in the original (parent) node is included in the cloned node; for example, the target variable, the roles and measurement levels for other variables and for the metadata sample are the same. You can also redefine the attributes of the cloned node.

If you did not clone the node, you would have to add a new *Input Data Source* node to the Diagram Workspace, set the node options, and create the metadata sample. If you are going to use the same data set often in the project, then this method takes longer than cloning an existing node.

Note: If you are going to use the same data set in several projects or diagrams, you can use the SAS Data Warehouse Administrator to set up the data sets, and use the Enterprise Miner Warehouse Add-ins for applying whatever measurement levels and roles you want in your data. Any users that use this data would pick up the metadata sample, along with the roles and measurement levels already assigned. △

To clone multiple nodes, add the nodes to a subdiagram node (see "Subdiagrams" on page 54) and then clone the subdiagram node.

To clone a node:

1 Select the node you want to clone (the parent node) in the Diagram Workspace.

2 Right–click the node and select the **Clone** pop-menu item.

The Clone Current Node window opens.

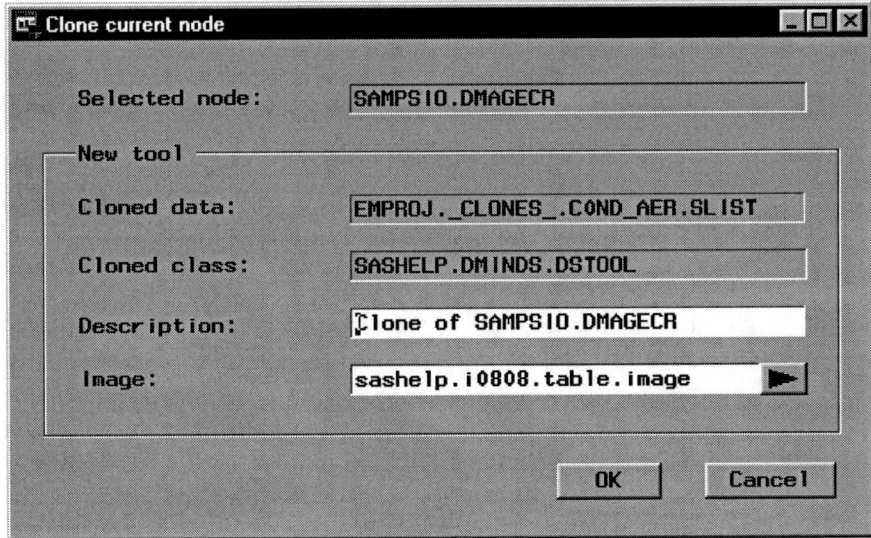

The Clone Current Node window lists the selected node and the following new tool (node) information:

- *Cloned data* — the SAS entry that contains the new node information.
- *Cloned class* — the catalog entry that identifies the parent node.
- *Description* — the name of the cloned node. By default, the description is set to "Clone of *node name*". You should type a new description in the entry field.
- *Image* — the icon that is used for the cloned node on the Tools Palette, Tools Bar, and the Diagram Workspace. By default, the parent node icon is used as the clone node icon. To change the icon image, select the arrow control and then select an icon from the list.

3 Type a node description in the **Description** field.

4 Select the **Image** arrow and choose a new icon image.

5 Select the [OK] button to return to the Diagram Workspace.

The node is added as a new custom tool entry on the Tools Palette of the Project Navigator.

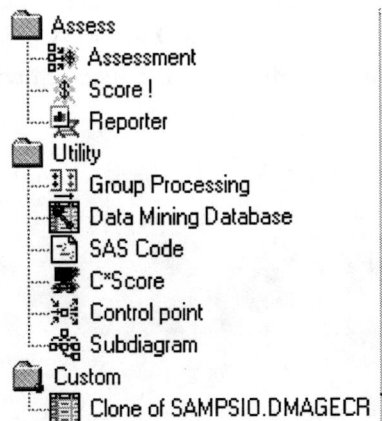

The cloned node (for this example, SAMPSIO.DMAGECR) can be used just like any other node on the Tools Palette. It can be redefined and/or connected to other nodes in a process flow, deleted, copied to the tools bar, and used in other process flow diagrams of the project.

Note: If you are working in a shared project environment, you should periodically refresh the Tools Palette in order to see and make use of clones that may have been created by other users. △

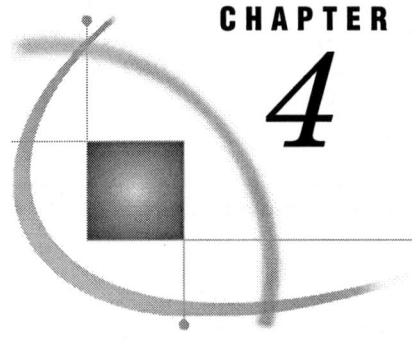

Process Flow Diagram Logic

Organization of Enterprise Miner Nodes

The nodes of Enterprise Miner are organized into categories of the *Sample, Explore, Modify, Model,* and *Assess* (SEMMA) data mining process. Notice that parts of the data mining process can be repeated; for example, you may want to explore data and plot data at several points in the process. Also, you may want to fit models, assess the models, refit the models and then reassess. In addition to the data mining tools, utility nodes are also provided. They enable you to submit SAS programming statements, to create data mining databases, to perform group processing, to define control points in the process flow diagram, and to create subdiagrams.

Sampling Nodes

- ☐ The *Input Data Source* node enables you to access SAS data sets and other types of data. This node reads data sources and defines their attributes for processing by Enterprise Miner. Meta information (the metadata sample) is automatically created for each variable when you import a data set with the Input Data Source node. Initial values are set for the measurement level and the model role for each variable. You can change these values if you are not satisfied with the automatic selections made by the node. Summary statistics are displayed for interval and class variables.

- ☐ The *Sampling* node enables you to take random, stratified random samples, and cluster samples of data sets. Sampling is recommended for extremely large databases because it can significantly decrease model training time. If the sample is sufficiently representative, then relationships found in the sample can be expected to generalize to the complete data set. The *Sampling* node writes the sampled observations to an output data set and saves the seed values that are used to generate the random numbers for the samples so that you may replicate the samples.

- □ The *Data Partition* node enables you to partition data sets into training, test, and validation data sets. The training data set is used for preliminary model fitting. The validation data set is used to monitor and tune the model weights during estimation and is also used for model assessment. The test data set is an additional hold-out data set that you can use for model assessment. This node uses simple random sampling, stratified random sampling, or user defined partitions to create partitioned data sets.

Exploring Nodes

- □ The *Distribution Explorer* node is an advanced visualization tool that enables you to quickly and easily explore large volumes of data in multidimensional histograms. You can view the distribution of up to three variables at a time with this node. When the variable is binary, nominal, or ordinal, you can select specific values to exclude from the chart. To exclude extreme values for interval variables, you can set a range cutoff. The node also generates summary statistics for the charting variables.

- □ The *Multiplot* node is another visualization tool that enables you to explore larger volumes of data graphically. Unlike the *Insight* or *Distribution Explorer* nodes, the *Multiplot* node automatically creates bar charts and scatter plots for the input and target variables without making several menu or window item selections. The code created by this node can be used to create graphs in a batch environment, whereas the *Insight* and *Distribution Explorer* nodes must be run interactively.

- □ The *Insight* node enables you to open a SAS/INSIGHT session. SAS/INSIGHT software is an interactive tool for data exploration and analysis. With it you explore data through graphs and analyses that are linked across multiple windows. You can analyze univariate distributions, investigate multivariate distributions, and fit explanatory models using generalized linear models.

- □ The *Association* node enables you to identify association relationships within the data. For example, if a customer buys a loaf of bread, how likely is the customer to also buy a gallon of milk? The node also enables you to perform sequence discovery if a time stamp variable (a sequence variable) is present in the data set. Binary sequences are constructed automatically, but you can use the event chain handler to construct longer sequences based on the patterns discovered by the algorithm.

- □ The *Variable Selection* node enables you to evaluate the importance of input variables in predicting or classifying the target variable. To preselect the important inputs, the node uses either an R-square or a chi-square selection (tree based) criterion. The R-square criterion enables you to remove variables in hierarchies, remove variables that have large percentages of missing values, and remove class variables that are based on the number of unique values. The variables that are not related to the target are set to a status of "rejected." Although rejected variables are passed to subsequent nodes in the process flow diagram, these variables are not used as model inputs by a more detailed modeling node, such as the *Neural Network* and *Tree* nodes. You can reassign the status of the input model variables to "rejected."

Modifying Nodes

- ☐ The *Data Set Attributes* node enables you to modify data set attributes, such as data set names, descriptions, and roles. You can also use this node to modify the metadata sample that is associated with a data set, and to specify target profiles for a target. An example of a useful *Data Set Attributes* application is to generate a data set in the *SAS Code* node and then modify its metadata sample with this node.

- ☐ The *Transform Variables* node enables you to transform variables: for example, you can transform variables by taking the square root of a variable or by taking the natural logarithm. Additionally, the node supports user-defined formulas for transformations and provides a visual interface for grouping interval-valued variables into buckets or quantiles. Transforming variables to similar scale and variability may improve the fit of models, and subsequently, the classification and prediction precision of fitted models.

- ☐ The *Filter Outliers* node enables you to identify and remove outliers from data sets. Checking for outliers is recommended as outliers may greatly affect modeling results and, subsequently, the classification and prediction precision of fitted models.

- ☐ The *Replacement* node enables you to impute (fill in) values for observations that have missing values. You can replace missing values for interval variables with the mean, median, midrange, or mid-minimum spacing, or with a distribution-based replacement. Alternatively, you can use a replacement M-estimator such as Tukey's biweight, Hubers, or Andrew's Wave. You can also estimate the replacement values for each interval input by using a tree-based imputation method. Missing values for class variables can be replaced with the most frequently occurring value, distribution based replacement, tree-based imputation, or a constant.

- ☐ The *Clustering* node enables you to segment your data; that is, it enables you to identify data observations that are similar in some way. Observations that are similar tend to be in the same cluster, and observations that are different tend to be in different clusters. The cluster identifier for each observation can be passed to other nodes for use as an input, ID, or target variable. It can also be passed as a group variable that enables you to automatically construct separate models for each group.

- ☐ The *SOM/Kohonen* node generates self organizing maps, Kohonen networks, and vector quantization networks. Essentially the node performs unsupervised learning in which it attempts to learn the structure of the data. As with the *Clustering* node, after the network maps have been created, the characteristics can be examined graphically using the results browser. The node provides the analysis results in the form of an interactive map illustrating the characteristics of the clusters. Furthermore, it provides a report indicating the importance of each variable.

Modeling Nodes

- ☐ The *Regression* node enables you to fit both linear and logistic regression models to your data. You can use continuous, ordinal, and binary target variables. You can use both continuous and discrete variables as inputs. The node supports the stepwise, forward, and backward selection methods. A point-and-click interaction builder enables you to create higher-order modeling terms.

□ The *Tree* node enables you to fit decision tree models to your data. The implementation includes features found in a variety of popular decision tree algorithms (for example, CHAID, CART, and C4.5). The node supports both automatic and interactive training. When you run the *Tree* node in automatic mode, it automatically ranks the input variables based on the strength of their contribution to the tree. This ranking may be used to select variables for use in subsequent modeling. You may override any automatic step with the option to define a splitting rule and delete explicit nodes or subtrees. Interactive training enables you to explore and evaluate a large set of trees as you develop them.

□ The *Neural Network* node enables you to construct, train, and validate multilayer feedforward neural networks. By default, the *Neural Network* node automatically constructs a multilayer feedforward network that has one hidden layer consisting of three neurons. In general, each input is fully connected to the first hidden layer, each hidden layer is fully connected to the next hidden layer, and the last hidden layer is fully connected to the output. The *Neural Network* node supports many variations of this general form.

□ The *Princomp/Dmneural* node enables you to fit an additive nonlinear model that uses the bucketed principal components as inputs to predict a binary or an interval target variable. The node also performs a principal components analysis and passes the scored principal components to the successor nodes.

□ The *User Defined Model* node enables you to generate assessment statistics using predicted values from a model that you built with the *SAS Code* node (for example, a logistic model using the SAS/STAT LOGISTIC procedure) or the *Variable Selection* node. The predicted values can also be saved to a SAS data set and then imported into the process flow with the *Input Data Source* node.

□ The *Ensemble* node creates a new model by averaging the posterior probabilities (for class targets) or the predicted values (for interval targets) from multiple models. The new model is then used to score new data. One common ensemble approach is to resample the training data and fit a separate model for each sample. The component models are then integrated by the *Ensemble* node to form a potentially stronger solution.

□ The *Forecasting* node enables you to forecast future values of the data based on its past behavior. In order to perform forecasting, you must have time series data, which is a set of variables collected over time periods, such as hours, days, weeks, or months. Internet, inventory, sales, and similar data are typical examples of time series data suitable for forecasting. You use the *Forecasting* node to fit time series data to an appropriate forecasting model. Once you select and fit a forecasting model, you generate forecast values for your variables of interest.

Note: These modeling nodes utilize a directory table facility, called the Model Manager, in which you can store and assess models on demand. The modeling nodes also enable you to modify the target profile(s) for a target variable. △

Assessing Nodes

□ The *Assessment* node provides a common framework for comparing models and predictions from any of the modeling nodes (*Regression, Tree, Neural Network,* and

User Defined Model nodes). The comparison is based on the expected and actual profits or losses that would result from implementing the model. The node produces the following charts that help to describe the usefulness of the model: lift, profit, return on investment, receiver operating curves, diagnostic charts, and threshold-based charts.

☐ The *Score* node enables you to generate and manage predicted values from a trained model. Scoring formulas are created for both assessment and prediction. Enterprise Miner generates and manages scoring formulas in the form of SAS DATA step code, which can be used in most SAS environments with or without Enterprise Miner.

☐ The *Reporter* node assembles the results from a process flow analysis into an HTML report that can be viewed with your favorite web browser. Each report contains header information, an image of the process flow diagram, and a separate subreport for each node in the flow. Reports are managed in the Reports tab of the Project Navigator.

Utility Nodes

☐ The *Group Processing* node enables you to perform group by-processing for class variables such as GENDER. You can also use this node to analyze multiple targets, and you can process the same data source repeatedly by setting the group processing mode to index.

☐ The *Data Mining Database* node enables you to create a data mining database (DMDB) for batch processing. For nonbatch processing, DMDBs are automatically created as they are needed.

☐ The *SAS Code* node enables you to incorporate new or existing SAS code into process flow diagrams. The ability to write SAS code enables you to include additional SAS procedures into your data mining analysis. You can also use a SAS DATA step to create customized scoring code, to conditionally process data, and to concatenate or to merge existing data sets. The node provides a macro facility to dynamically reference data sets used for training, validation, testing, or scoring and variables, such as input, target, and predict variables. After you run the *SAS Code* node, the results and the data sets can then be exported for use by subsequent nodes in the diagram.

☐ The *C Score* node produces a plain text output file based on Enterprise Miner input from a process flow analysis. The output file can be specified by the SAS filename CSCORE. If no output file is specified or the output file can not be opened, output is sent to the SAS log. The C code generated by *C Score* represents the SAS data step code input. *C Score* should support all valid targets for *SOM/Kohonen*, *Variable Selection*, *Neural Network*, *Regression*, *Sampling*, *Tree*, and *Clustering*.

☐ The *Control Point* node enables you to establish a control point to reduce the number of connections that are made in process flow diagrams. For example, suppose three *Input Data Source* nodes are to be connected to three modeling nodes. If no *Control Point* node is used, then nine connections are required to connect all of the *Input Data Source* nodes to all of the modeling nodes. However, if a *Control Point* node is used, only six connections are required.

☐ The *Subdiagram* node enables you to group a portion of a process flow diagram into a subdiagram. For complex process flow diagrams, you may want to create subdiagrams to better design and control the process flow.

Subdiagrams

Some process flow diagrams may be quite complex. To assist in controlling the process flow, you can create subdiagrams and collapse a set of nodes and connections into a single node icon. Subdiagrams can be opened to display the complete structure of the process flow diagram.

Note: You cannot uncondense the nodes in a subdiagram. △

There are two major approaches to creating subdiagrams:

- You know in advance that you will use a subdiagram. First, you add a *Subdiagram* node, and then add nodes within the subdiagram. See "Subdiagram Example 1" on page 54.
- You may realize later that if a particular set of nodes were condensed into a subdiagram, then the process flow would be much easier to control. See "Subdiagram Example 2" on page 56.

Subdiagram Example 1

Suppose you want a process flow diagram to contain a subdiagram for the following nodes: *Sampling, Data Partition, Filter Outliers,* and *Transform Variables.*
To create a subdiagram for these nodes, follow these steps:

1 Add and define any predecessor nodes from the Tools Palette that you do not want as part of the subdiagram to the Diagram Workspace.

2 Add a *Subdiagram* node to the process flow diagram.

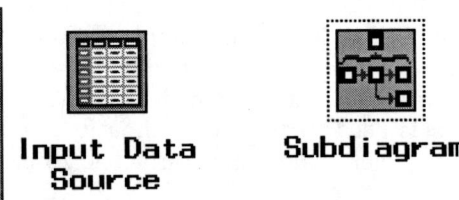

Input Data Source   **Subdiagram**

3 Connect the predecessor node to the *Subdiagram* node and then open the *Subdiagram* node by double-clicking on the node icon. Alternatively, you can right-click on the node icon and select the **Open** menu item.

   Within the *Subdiagram* node are *Enter* and *Exit* nodes, which by default are connected.

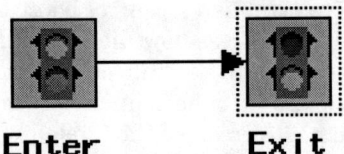

Enter   **Exit**

4 Cut the connection between the *Enter* and *Exit* nodes by right-clicking on the connection arrow and selecting the **Delete** pop-up menu item.

Note: The *Enter* and *Exit* nodes are connected to allow for independent subdiagrams. △

5 Move the *Enter* and *Exit* nodes to the appropriate locations in the process flow diagram, and then add and connect the desired nodes.

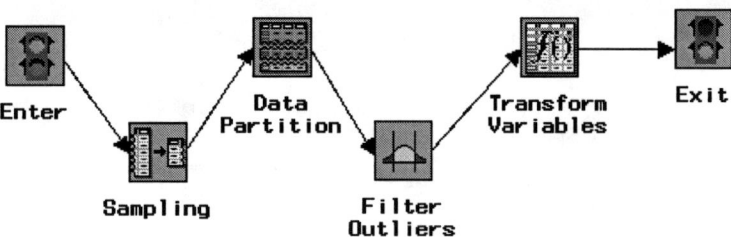

6 Condense the subdiagram, by using the **View** pull-down menu (or the pop-up menu) to select the **Up One Level** menu item.

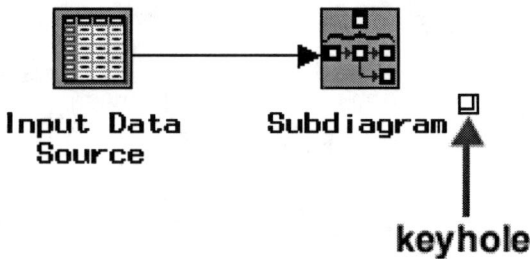

Note: When a subdiagram has been defined, a key hole appears beside the Subdiagram node. To open the subdiagram, you can select the key hole or you can double-click on the node icon. △

7 Position the *Subdiagram* node in the appropriate location within the process flow diagram, and then connect the *Subdiagram* node to the appropriate nodes.

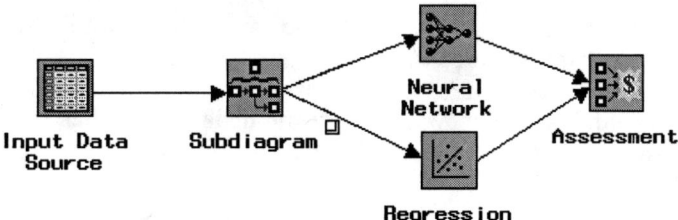

This example process flow diagram has an *Input Data Source* node that is connected to the *Subdiagram* node, which in turn connects to a *Neural Network* node and a *Regression* node. The resulting models are compared and assessed in an *Assessment* node.

Note: You can clone"Cloning a Node" on page 45 the example *Subdiagram* node if you need to use it often in the project. △

Subdiagram Example 2

In this example, you are developing a process flow diagram:

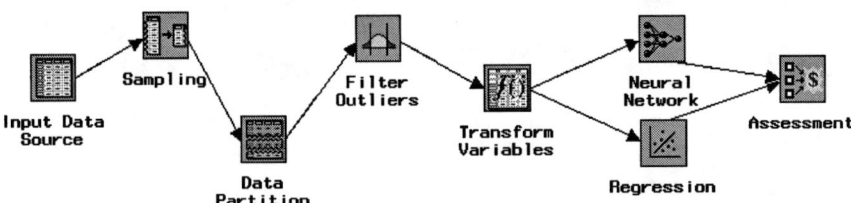

You realize that you could create a subdiagram to contain the following nodes: *Sampling*, *Data Partition*, *Filter Outliers*, and *Transform Variables*. By condensing these nodes into a subdiagram, you can more easily view other portions of the complete process flow diagram. To create a subdiagram for these nodes, follow these steps:

1 Select the first node to be included in the subdiagram. A box appears around the selected node (for this example, the *Sampling* node).

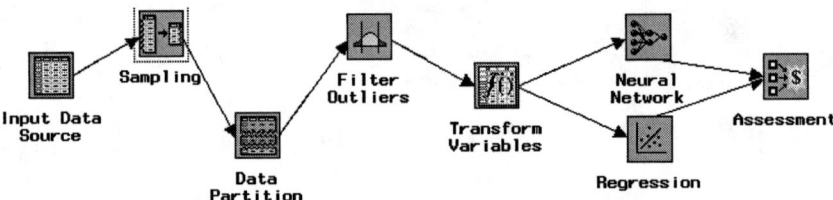

2 Place the mouse pointer on the arrow that connects the node selected in step 1 and the second node to be included in the subdiagram, then CTRL-click or SHIFT-click on the arrow. The selected arrow changes from an arrow to a line segment.

3 CTRL-click or SHIFT-click on the second node that you want to include in the subdiagram.

4 Repeat steps 2 and 3 until all nodes and arrows that you want to place in the subdiagram are selected. Note that for large process flow diagrams containing many nodes only the nodes and arrows that are selected are used to create the subdiagram.

Note: As an alternative to steps 1–4, you can "rubber band" the nodes and arrows to be selected. That is, place the mouse pointer in the process flow diagram near the nodes to be included in the subdiagram (where "near" is on one side of the set of node icons and either above or below the node icons), click and hold the left mouse button, and stretch the "rubber band" around the appropriate node icons. △

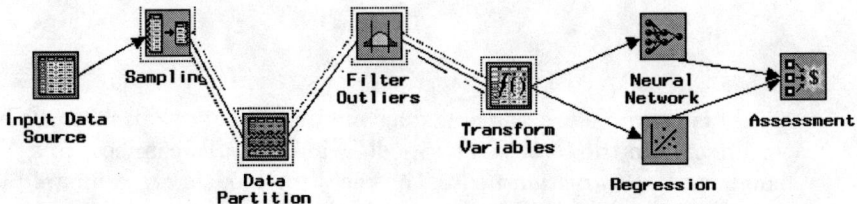

5 Use the main menu to choose

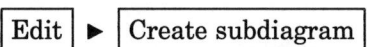

A dialog box appears that asks you to verify that the currently selected nodes and arrows are to be condensed into a subdiagram.

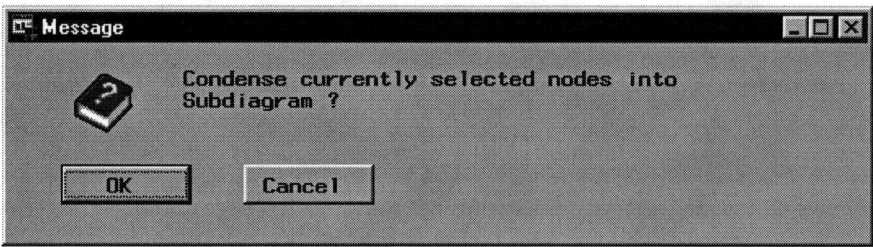

If you click the Cancel button, then the subdiagram is not created. If you click the OK button, then the subdiagram is created, and a subdiagram node icon replaces the selected nodes and arrows.

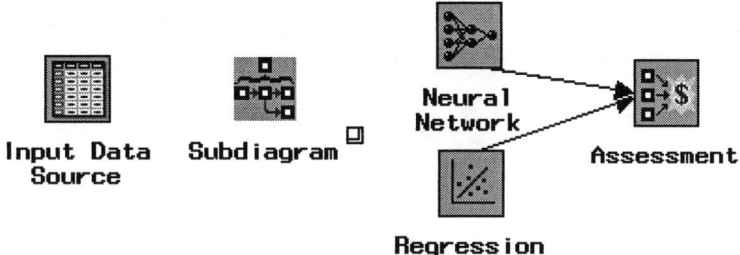

6 To open the *Subdiagram* node, double-click on the node icon or select the key hole.

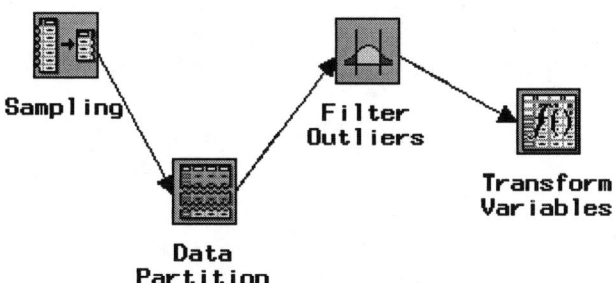

7 Add endpoints (a pair of nodes consisting of an *Enter* node and an *Exit* node) to the subdiagram to indicate where information enters the subdiagram and where it exits the subdiagram. (To add endpoints, right-click on an open area of the Diagram Workspace and select the **Add endpoints** pop-up menu item.) By default, the *Enter* node is connected to the *Exit* node. Cut the connection between the *Enter* and *Exit* nodes, and then position the *Enter* node to the left of the subdiagram (so that it precedes the subdiagram) and the *Exit* node to the right of the subdiagram (so that it follows the subdiagram). Connect the *Enter* node to the subdiagram (the connection arrow should point to the subdiagram), and connect the subdiagram to the *Exit* node (the connection arrow should point to the *Exit* node).

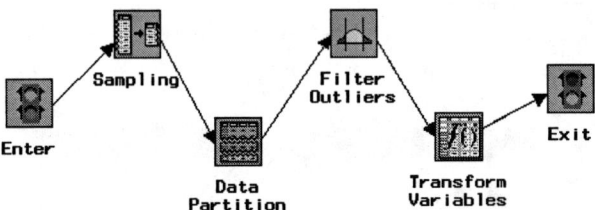

8 Condense the subdiagram by using the **View** pull-down menu (or the pop-up menu) to select the **Up One Level** menu item.

9 Connect the *Subdiagram* node to the appropriate nodes. In this example, an *Input Data Source* node passes information to the *Subdiagram* node, which passes information to the *Regression* and *Neural Network* nodes, which in turn pass information to the *Assessment* node.

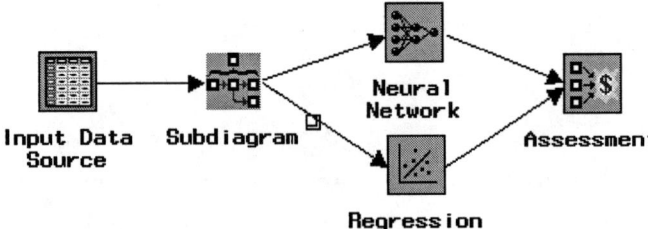

You cannot uncondense the nodes in a subdiagram. There is no restriction on how many *Subdiagram* nodes you can nest in the process flow diagram.

Usage Rules for Nodes

Following are some general rules that govern the placement of nodes in a process flow diagram:

□ The *Input Data Source* node cannot be preceded by any other nodes.

□ All nodes except the *Input Data Source* and *SAS Code* nodes must be preceded by a node that exports a data set.

□ The *SAS Code* node can be defined in any stage of the process flow diagram. It does not require an input data set that is defined in the *Input Data Source* node. If you create a SAS data set with code you write in the *SAS Code* node (for example, a data set that contains target and predict variables), you can use a successor *Data Set Attributes* node to assign model roles to the variables in the SAS data set.

□ The *Assessment* node must be preceded by one or more modeling nodes.

□ The *Score* node must be preceded by a node that produces score code. For example, the modeling nodes produce score code.

□ The *Data Set Attributes* can only have one node preceding it.

□ The *Ensemble* node must be preceded by a modeling node.

□ The *Reporter* node generates HTML reports for all of the predecessor nodes. It does not generate reports for the successor nodes. When you run the flow from the *Reporter* node, Enterprise Miner makes a first pass through the flow to analyze the data. After the analysis is complete, Enterprise Miner makes a second pass to generate the HTML reports. The node icons are colored green during the analysis pass and yellow during the reporting pass.

☐ You can have one *Group Processing* node per process flow. Group processing occurs when you run the process flow path. The *Group Processing* node can be connected to any successor node, but the only nodes that accumulate results from each pass are the modeling nodes and the *Score* node.

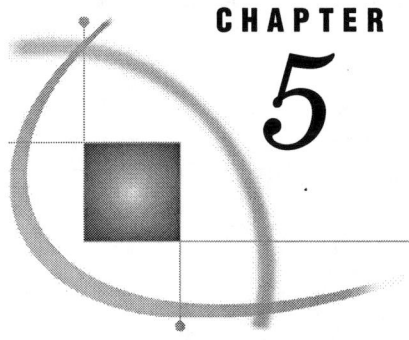

CHAPTER

5

Common Features among Nodes

Functionality

The following list of functionalities are common to all or most nodes.

☐ If you make changes to a node and then close it, a message window displays the following message: "Do you want to Save the Changes to *node name*". If you select the ⟨Yes⟩ button, then the current settings of the tool are saved, and the tool is closed. If you select the ⟨No⟩ button, then the current settings are *not* saved, and the tool is closed. If you select the ⟨Cancel⟩ button, then the message window is canceled, and the node is not closed. The message window does not appear if you did not make any changes to the node settings.

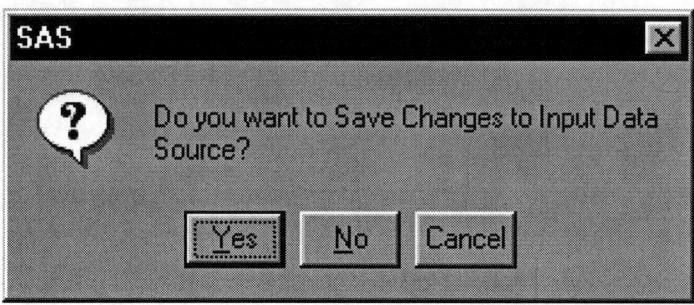

☐ When a node is run, information flows through the process flow diagram. A green box appears around each node as it processes the incoming information. If a node cannot process the information, then a red box appears around it, and you should check the Message Panel, the Message window, or the Log window and adjust the settings as necessary.

☐ When the analysis for the selected node has run, a message window prompts you to view the results. Select the ⟨Yes⟩ button to close the message window and open the results in the Results browser. Select the ⟨No⟩ button to close the message window and return to the Diagram Workspace.

Data Tab

A Data tab is contained in most nodes, and it displays the names for the available predecessor data sets, which can include some or all of the training, validation, test, and score data sets. You can select a predecessor data set from this list.

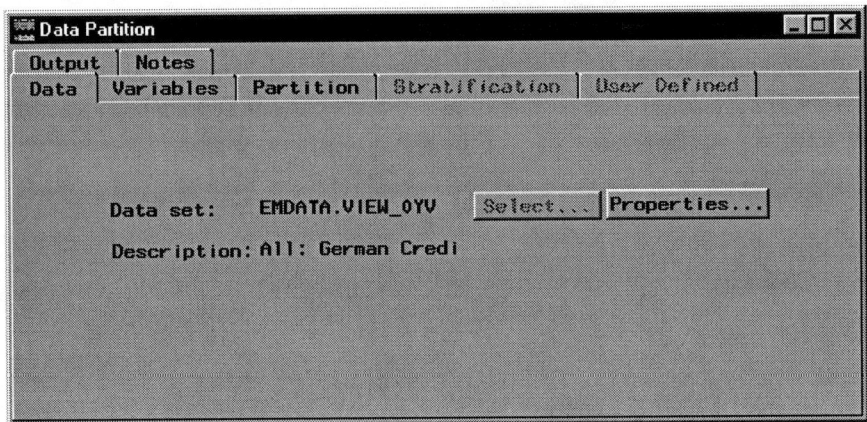

To select another data set that is exported from a node that precedes the current node, click the Select button. An explorer interface opens that enables you to find and select another data set. The Select button is grayed out if only one data set exporting node precedes the current node.

Note: Many nodes contain training, test, validation, and score radio buttons on the tab that enable you to assign a specific data set to each of these data set roles. △

To view administrative information about the data set, click the Properties button. The administrative information is the data set name, label, type, date created, date last modified, number of columns, number of rows, and number of deleted rows.

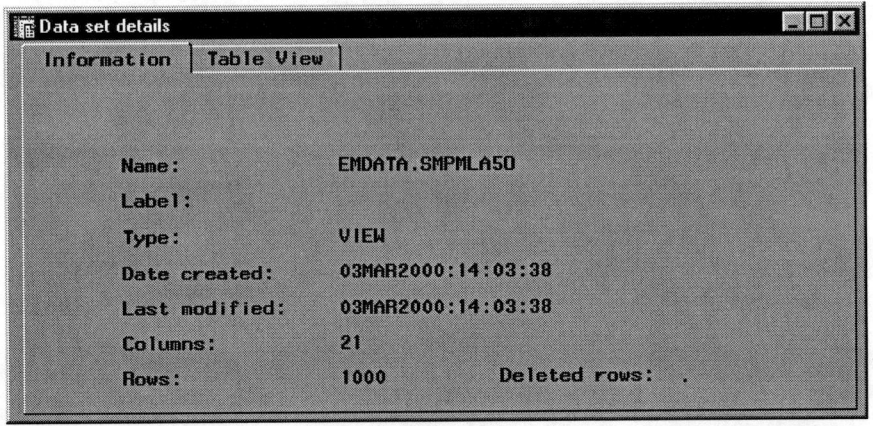

To see a table view of the data, select the Table View tab.

Variables Tab

A Variables tab is contained in most nodes, and it displays the following attributes about the variables:

□ The names of the variables in the input data set. The values in the Name column are protected.

□ The status of the variables, which can be **use** or **don't use**. You can change the status of a variable in one of the sampling or modeling nodes. For most explore nodes, you cannot change the variable's status. To change the status of a variable, follow these steps:

    1 Right-click on the appropriate cell of the **Status** column.

    2 Select the **Set Status** pop-up menu item.

    3 Select the appropriate status (either **don't use** or **use**).

Note: The Variables tab of the *Input Data Source* node does not contain a **Status** column. To assign the rejected model role to a variable, right-click on the appropriate cell of the **Model Role** column to open a pop-up menu. Select the **Set Model Role** menu item and then select the **rejected** menu item. You use this same protocol to assign the rejected role to variables in the Manual Selection tab of the *Variable Selection* node. △

Here is an example display of the Variables tab of the *Input Data Source* node:

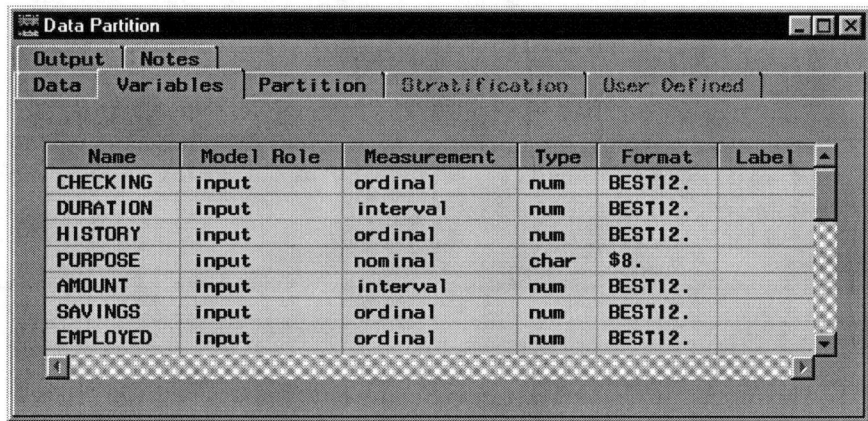

In this node, the Variables tab contains the following columns:

□ **Name** — the variable name.

□ **Model Role** — the variable model role. Examples of model roles include cost, freq, ID, input, predict, rejected, sequence, target, and trial (see the for definitions of these roles). The role of a variable is automatically assigned in the *Input Data Source* node based on the information in the metadata sample. You can change the role that is automatically assigned to a variable.

□ **Measurement** — the measurement type of the variable. Examples of measurement type include binary, interval, ordinal, and nominal. The measurement type of variables is automatically assigned in the *Input Data Source* node based on the information in the metadata sample.

□ **Type** — either character (char) or numeric (num). The variable type is displayed in the *Input Data Source* node, but it cannot be changed (the values in this column are protected).

□ **Format** — the format of the variable. Examples of formats include $18. (18 characters) and BEST12. (12-digit numeric). The variable formats are assigned in the *Input Data Source* node.

□ **Variable Label** — the descriptive variable label, which is assigned in the *Input Data Source* node. To change the label for a variable, type a new value in the appropriate cell of the Variable Label column.

You can sort by clicking on the column header buttons. Successive clicks on the header toggle the sort between ascending and descending order.

Subsetting (displaying a subset of the variables) can be performed for the variable attributes of status, model role, measurement, and type:

1 Right-click in any row of the attribute you want to subset. A pop-up menu appears.

2 Select the item **Subset by <attribute>** and a selection list box appears containing the set of attribute values that are available for subsetting.

3 Select the appropriate attribute values for subsetting.

4 To accept the selections and display the subsetting, click $\boxed{\text{OK}}$. To cancel the subsetting dialog box, click $\boxed{\text{Cancel}}$.

To find a value within a column, follow these steps:

1 Right-click on the column heading or a cell within the column and select the **Find <colname>** pop-up menu item. The Find <colname> window opens, which is modeled after the Find dialog in Internet Explorer.

2 Type the text in the **Find <attribute>** field.

3 Specify the search direction (up or down) and whether you want the text to match the whole field.

4 Click $\boxed{\text{OK}}$.

If Enterprise Miner finds the text in the column you are searching for, and in the direction you specified, it will then move the row containing the text to the top of the table. If it does not, it displays "No match detected" at the bottom of the screen and issues a beep signal.

Notes Tab

The Notes tab enables you to type and store notes about the project, the analysis, the results, and so on. When you run a process flow that contains a *Reporter* node, the notes are assembled into the resulting HTML report.

Results browser

The Results browser enables you to view the results of running a node that generates results. To open the Results browser, follow these steps:

□ If the node is closed,

   1 right–click on the node icon and select the **Results** pop-up menu item.

   2 from the main menu, choose

      $\boxed{\text{Actions}}$ ▶ $\boxed{\text{Results}}$

□ If the node is open,

   1 select the Results browser tool icon on the Toolbox.

2 from the main menu, choose

| Tools | ▶ | Results browser |

Note: After you run particular nodes, such as the *Tree* or the *Data Partition* node, a message window displays that asks you if you want to view the results. Click Yes to open the Results browser. △

Viewing and Setting Node Defaults

To view the properties for any node, right-click on the node icon in the Tools Palette of the Project Navigator, or click the Tools Bar at the top of the SAS Enterprise Miner window, and select the **Properties** pop-up menu item. The Properties *<Node Name>* window opens, which summarizes the node properties.

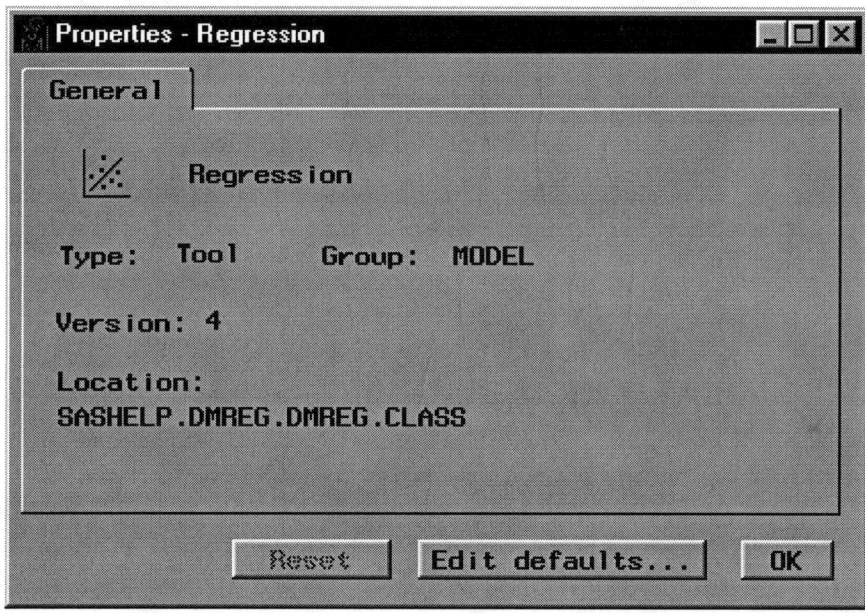

Note: The Reset button is dimmed if the node is set to the original defaults. △

You can customize the default settings for the following nodes:

- ☐ *Data Partition*
- ☐ *Sampling*
- ☐ *Insight*
- ☐ *Association*
- ☐ *Variable Selection*
- ☐ *Replacement*
- ☐ *Clustering*
- ☐ *SOM / Kohonen*
- ☐ *Regression*
- ☐ *Tree*
- ☐ *Neural Network*
- ☐ *Assessment*

□ *Score*

□ *Group Processing*

To customize the default node settings, select the [Edit defaults] button in the Properties window and make the desired selections in the tabs of the Defaults window:

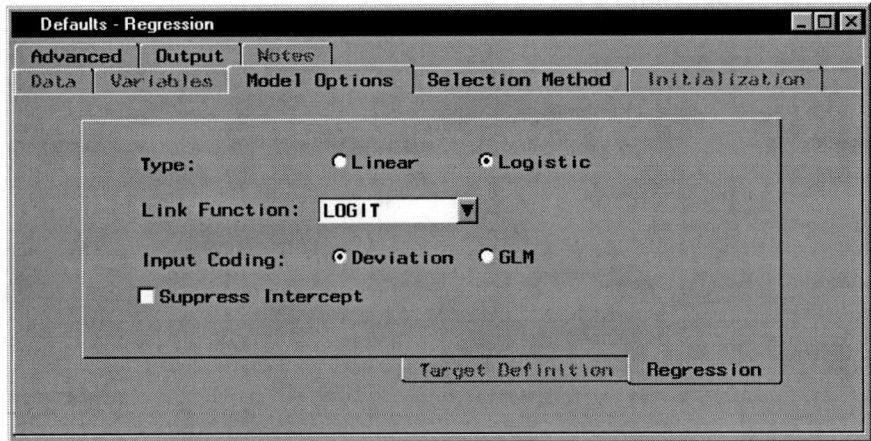

After you have set the node defaults, close the Defaults window to return to the Properties window.

To reset the node to the original defaults, click the [Reset] button.

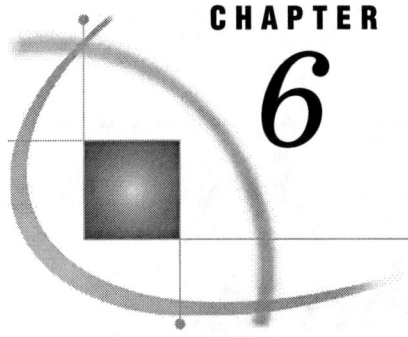

CHAPTER

6

Data Structure Examples

Types of Data Structures

Data structures for data-mining data sets and data marts include the following:

- [ ] regression data (see"Regression Data" on page 68), which has the following characteristics:
  - [ ] one observation per customer.
  - [ ] a binary target (dependent) variable, a continuous (interval) target variable, or both. Often only one target variable is modeled per run, but you can use a *Group Processing* node to model multiple targets. An example of a binary target variable is purchase or no-purchase, which is useful for modeling customer profiles. An example of a continuous (interval) target variable is value of purchase, which is useful for modeling the best customers for particular products, catalogs, or sales campaigns.
  - [ ] many or few input variables, which can contain ID (identification) variables, demographic data, history or previous purchases, and so forth.
  - [ ] cross-sectional data, which is data collected across multiple customers, products, geographic regions, and so on, but typically not across multiple time periods.
- [ ] associations discovery data (see "Association Discovery Data" on page 70), also called basket analysis data, which is a common data structure of online transaction processing systems (OLTPs). Such data structures have the following characteristics:
  - [ ] multiple observations per customer. The data set must contain a separate observation for each transaction.
  - [ ] a target (dependent) variable – often a class variable that has a level for each product.
  - [ ] one or more ID variables to identify the customers.
  - [ ] a sequence variable if you are performing a sequence discovery. The sequence variable identifies the ordering of the purchases.
- [ ] time-series data analysis, which is more fully supported in SAS/ETS (econometric and time series) software. Analyses using SAS/ETS procedures can be submitted in the *SAS Code* node.

□ time-series cross-sectional (panel) data analysis, which is more fully supported in the SAS/ETS and SAS/STAT products. Analyses using SAS/ETS and SAS/STAT procedures can be submitted in the *SAS Code* node.

Regression Data

An example of the regression data is shown in the following display:

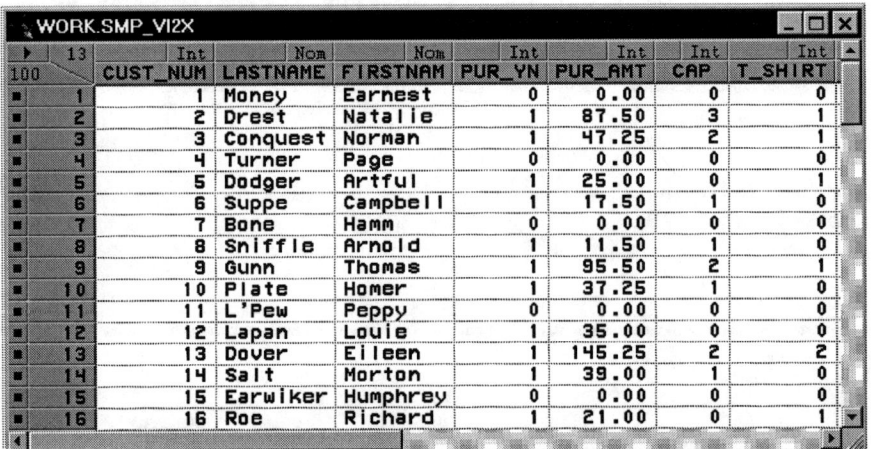

Note: Some of the variables in the example data set are hidden in this SAS/INSIGHT display. △

Following are all of the variables in the example data set:

□ CUST_NUM, customer number, an ID (identification) variable.

□ LASTNAME, the customer's last name.

□ FIRSTNAM, the customer's first name.

□ PUR_YN, a binary variable where "0" indicates no purchase and "1" indicates purchase.

□ PUR_AMT, a continuous variable that contains the amount of purchase.

□ CAP, a continuous variable that contains the number of baseball caps purchased.

□ T_SHIRT, a continuous variable that contains the number of t-shirts purchased.

□ SW_SHIRT, a continuous variable that contains the number of sweatshirts purchased.

□ MARRIED, a binary variable where "0" indicates the customer is not currently married and "1" indicates that the customer is married.

□ CHILDREN, a binary variable where "0" indicates the customer has no children and "1" indicates that the customer has children.

□ SALARY, a continuous variable that contains the customer's annual salary in thousands.

□ OWN_RENT, a binary variable where "0" indicates the customer rents a home and "1" indicates that the customer owns a home.

□ PREV_PUR, a binary variable where "0" indicates the customer has not made previous purchases and "1" indicates that the customer has made previous purchases.

For a regression model using PUR_AMT as the target variable and MARRIED, CHILDREN, SALARY, OWN_RENT, and PREV_PUR as input variables, the Variables tab of the *Input Data Source* node would appear as follows:

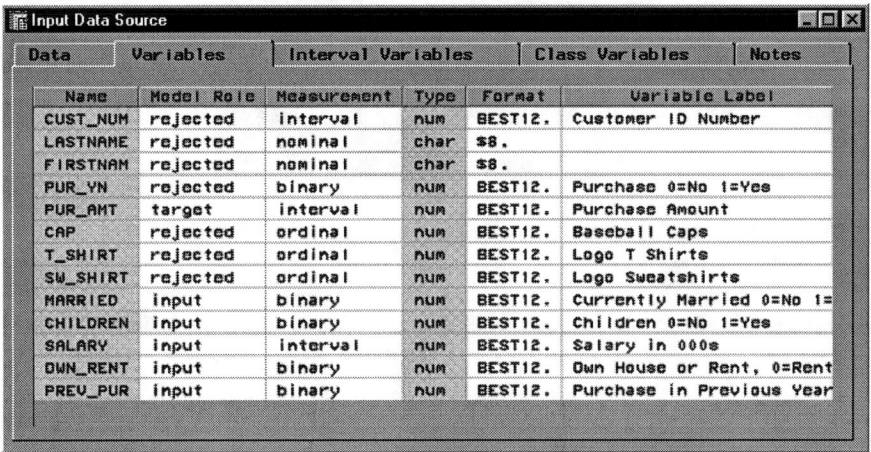

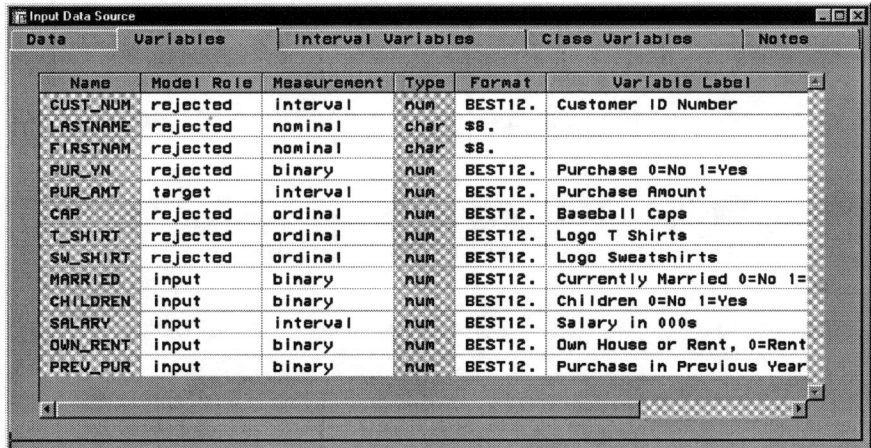

Note that the binary variable PUR_YN has been excluded from the analysis along with six other variables.

The process flow diagram might be as follows:

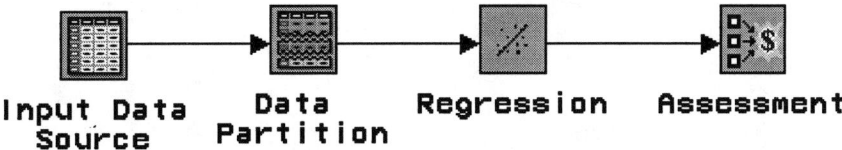

Input Data Source → Data Partition → Regression → Assessment

After you run the process flow diagram, you can view the regression results by right-clicking on the *Regression* node icon and selecting the **Results** pop-up menu item.

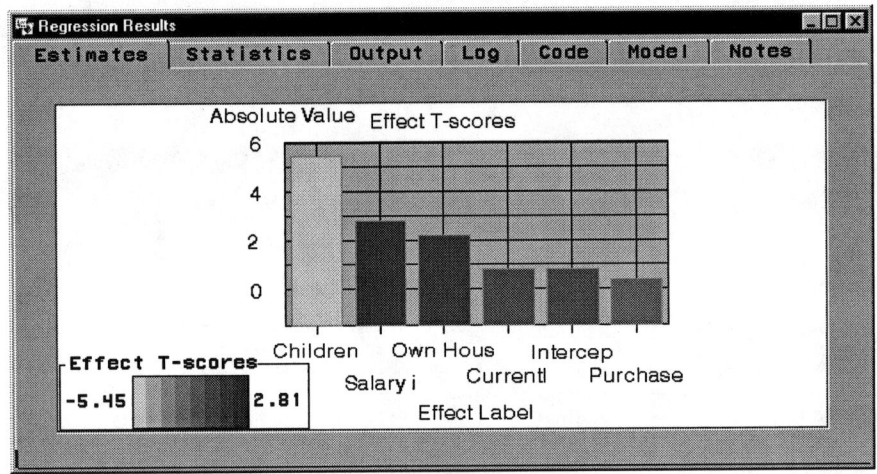

You can also open the *Assessment* node to create assessment charts that indicate the usefulness of the model.

Association Discovery Data

An example of association discovery data is shown in the following display:

```
OUTPUT - (Untitled)                                        _ □ ✕
            Data for Association Discovery
                                                     15:51

    CUST_NUM      LASTNAME       FIRSTNAM       PRODUCT

         98       Arya           How            cap
         98       Arya           How            tshirt
         98       Arya           How            tshirt
         95       Aska           Al             sweatshr
         37       Balaya         Jim            tshirt
         72       Beach          Sandy          tshirt
         72       Beach          Sandy          sweatshr
         72       Beach          Sandy          cap
         82       Bellum         Sara           cap
         82       Bellum         Sara           tshirt
         19       Bloom          Leopold        cap
         19       Bloom          Leopold        sweatshr
         22       Bloom          Molly          cap
         22       Bloom          Molly          sweatshr
         41       Boat           John           tshirt
          7       Bone           Hamm           sweatshr
          7       Bone           Hamm           cap
          7       Bone           Hamm           cap
          7       Bone           Hamm           tshirt
         49       Bone           T.             cap
         49       Bone           T.             tshirt
         35       Boot           Jack           cap
         35       Boot           Jack           tshirt
         69       Briecant       Lou            cap
         69       Briecant       Lou            cap
```

This output contains the following variables:

- CUST_NUM, customer number, an ID (identification) variable.
- LASTNAME, the customer's last name.
- FIRSTNAM, the customer's first name.
- PRODUCT, a nominal (class) variable that contains the product purchased.

For an association discovery analysis (basket analysis) using PRODUCT as the target variable and CUST_NUM as the ID (identification) variable, the Variables tab of the *Input Data Source* node would appear as follows:

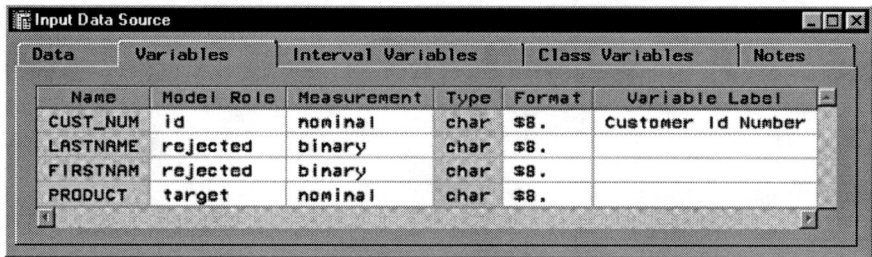

Note: The values in the **Name** and **Type** column are grayed out because they are protected fields. △

The process flow diagram appears as follows:

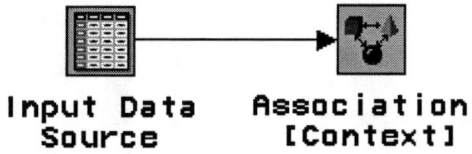

Input Data Source   **Association [Context]**

The *Association* node also enables you to perform sequence discovery. Sequence discovery goes one step further than association discovery by taking into account the ordering of the relationship among items. For example, "Of those customers who purchase a new computer, 25% of them will purchase a laser printer in the next quarter." To perform sequence discovery, you must also assign a sequence model role to a time stamp variable. For information about sequence discovery, see the online documentation for the *Association* node.

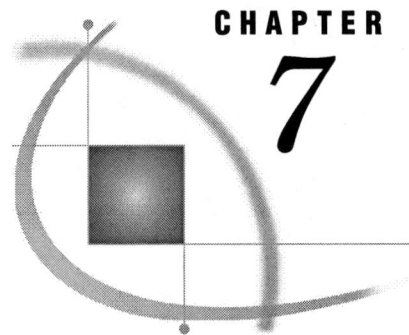

Example Process Flow Diagram

Process Flow Scenario

The following credit scoring flow is designed to get you started building Enterprise Miner process flow diagrams. Several key features of Enterprise Miner are demonstrated:

- □ specifying the input data set
- □ defining a target profile for the target
- □ creating partitioned data sets
- □ transforming variables
- □ supervised modeling, which includes a logistic regression model, a tree model, and a neural network model.
- □ assessing the models
- □ scoring new data.

For more detailed information about the nodes used in this example, read the Enterprise Miner Nodes online documentation or attend one of the data mining courses offered by the Education Division of SAS Institute.

In the following scenario, you want to build models that predict the credit status of credit applicants. The champion model (score card) will be used to determine whether or not to extend credit to new applicants. The aim is to anticipate and reduce charge-offs and defaults, which management has deemed are too high.

The input data set that is used to train the models is named SAMPSIO.DMAGECR (the German Credit benchmark data set). This data set is stored in the SAS Sample Library. It consists of 1,000 past applicants and their resulting credit rating ("GOOD" or "BAD"). The binary target (dependent, response variable) is named GOOD_BAD. The other 20 variables in the data set will serve as model inputs (independent, explanatory variables).

VARIABLE	ROLE	LEVEL	DESCRIPTION
CHECKING	input	ordinal	Checking account status
DURATION	input	interval	Duration in months
HISTORY	input	ordinal	Credit history
PURPOSE	input	nominal	Purpose
AMOUNT	input	interval	Credit amount
SAVINGS	input	ordinal	Savings account/bonds
EMPLOYED	input	ordinal	Present employment since
INSTALLP	input	interval	Installment rate as % of disposable income
MARITAL	input	nominal	Personal status and sex
COAPP	input	nominal	Other debtors/guarantors
RESIDENT	input	interval	Present residence since
PROPERTY	input	nominal	Property
AGE	input	interval	Age in years
OTHER	input	nominal	Other installment plans
HOUSING	input	nominal	Housing
EXISTCR	input	interval	Number of existing credits at this bank
JOB	input	ordinal	Job title
DEPENDS	input	interval	Number of dependents
TELEPHON	input	binary	Telephone
FOREIGN	input	binary	Foreign worker
GOOD_BAD	target	binary	Good or bad credit rating

Note: For more information about the variable values, see the Variable Layout for "SAMPSIO.DMAGECR (German Credit Data Set)" on page 117. △

Sixty percent of the data in the SAMPSIO.DMAGECR data set will be employed to train the models (the training data). The remainder of the data will be used to adjust the models for overfitting with regards to the training data and to compare the models (the validation data). The models will be judged primarily on their assessed profitability and accuracy and secondarily on their interpretability.

Each of the modeling nodes can make a decision for each case in the data to be scored, based on numerical consequences specified via a decision matrix and cost variables or constant costs. In Enterprise Miner, a decision matrix is defined as part of the target profile for the target. For this example flow, you want to define a loss matrix that adjusts the models for the expected losses for each decision (accept or reject an applicant). Michie, Spiegelhalter, and Taylor propose the following loss matrix for the SAMPSIO.DMAGECR data set:

| Target Values | Decisions: | |
	Accept	Reject
Good	$0	$1
Bad	$5	$0

Note: Michie, D., Spiegelhalter, D.J., and Taylor, C.C., eds. (1994), *Machine Learning, Neural and Statistical Classification*, NY: Ellis Harwood. p. 153. △

The rows of the matrix represent the target values and the columns represent the decisions. For the loss matrix, accepting a bad credit risk is five times worse than rejecting a good credit risk. However, this loss matrix also says that you cannot make any money no matter what you do, so the results may be difficult to interpret. In fact, if you accept a good credit risk, you will make money, that is, you will have a negative loss. And if you reject an applicant (good or bad), there will be no profit or loss aside from the cost of processing the application, which will be ignored. Hence it would be more realistic to subtract one from the first row of the matrix to give a more realistic loss matrix:

| Target Values | Decisions: | |
	Accept	Reject
Good	$-1	0
Bad	$5	0

This loss matrix will yield the same decisions and the same model selections as the first matrix, but the summary statistics for the second matrix will be easier to interpret.

For a categorical target, such as GOOD_BAD, each modeling node can estimate posterior probabilities for each class, which are defined as conditional probabilities of the classes given the input variables. By default, Enterprise Miner computes the posterior probabilities under the assumption that the prior probabilities are proportional to the frequencies of the classes in the training data set. For this example, you need to specify the correct prior probabilities in the decision data set, because the sample proportions of the classes in the training data set differ substantially from the proportions in the operational data set to be scored. The training data set that you will use for modeling contains 70% and 30% good and bad credit risk applicants, respectively. The actual assumed proportion of good-to-bad credit risk applicants in the score data set is 90% and 10%, respectively. By specifying the correct priors in the target profile for GOOD_BAD, the posterior probabilities will be correctly adjusted no matter what the proportions are in the training data set.

Once the most appropriate model for screening bad credit applicants is determined, the scoring code will be deployed to a fictitious score data set named SAMPSIO.DMAGESCR. It contains 75 new applicants. This data set is also stored in the SAS Sample Library. Scoring new data that does not contain the target is the end result of most data mining applications.

Follow these steps to create this process flow diagram:

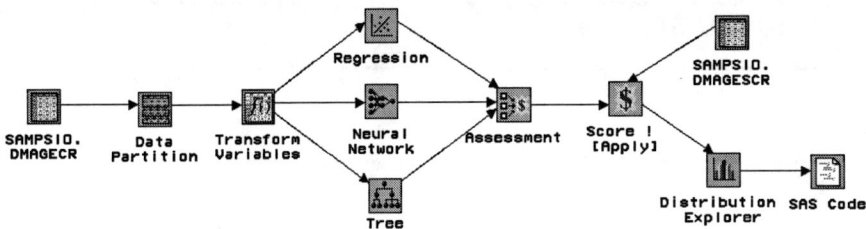

CAUTION:

Example results may differ. Enterprise Miner Version 4.0 was still under development when this process flow diagram was constructed. Your process flow diagram results may differ from the results shown in this example. However, the overall scope of the analysis will be the same. △

1. Creating a New Local Project

1 To start Enterprise Miner, you must first have a session of SAS running. You open Enterprise Miner from within SAS by typing **miner** in the command-line bar (found in the upper left corner) in an open SAS session. Enterprise Miner should start and load itself inside the main SAS window.

2 Use the **File** pull-down menu from the SAS / Enterprise Miner window to select

 New ► Project

The Create New Project window opens.

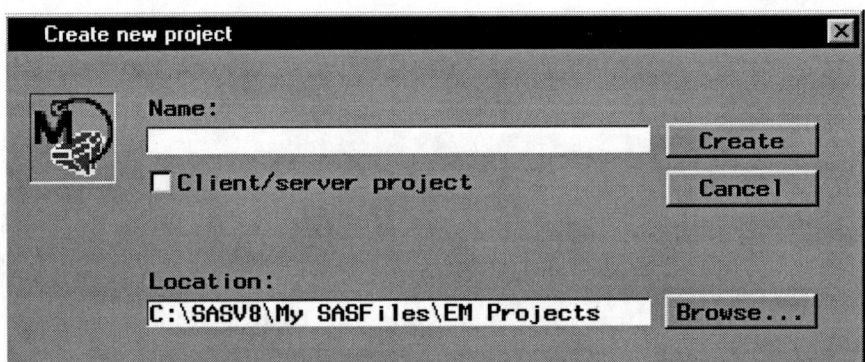

3 Type the project name in the **Name** entry field.

4 A project location will be suggested. You can type a different location for storing the project in the **Location** field, or use the Browse button to search for a location using a GUI interface.

5 After setting your project location, select Create. Enterprise Miner creates the project which contains a default diagram labeled "Untitled."

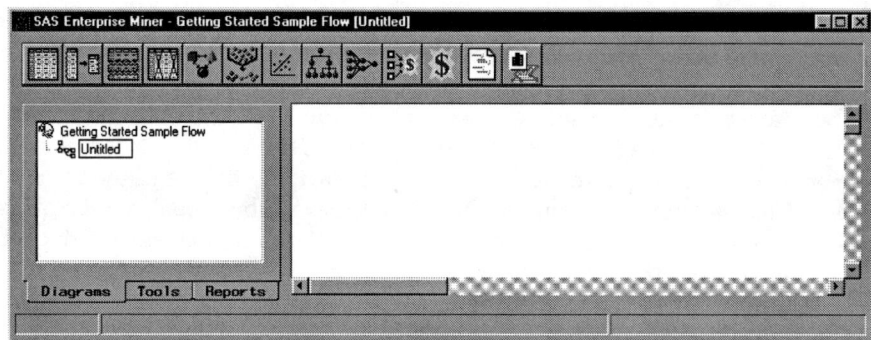

6 To rename the diagram, right-click on the diagram icon or label in the Diagrams tab of the Project Navigator and select **Rename**. Type a new diagram name.

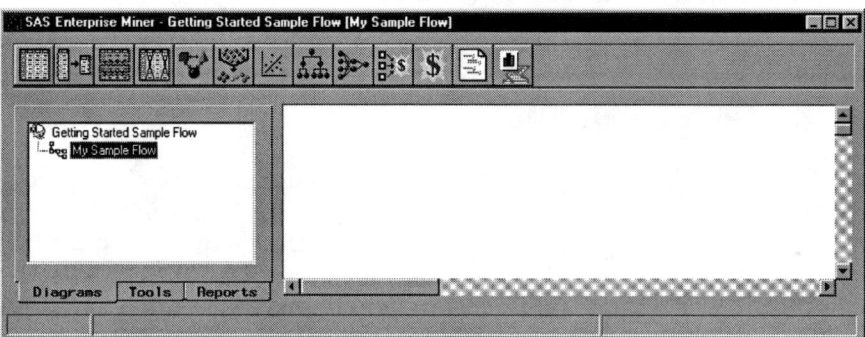

2. Defining the Input Data Set

1 Drag and drop an *Input Data Source* node from the Tools Palette of the Project Navigator or the toolbox to the Diagram Workspace.

2 To open the node, double-click on the node icon.

3 Type SAMPSIO.DMAGECR in the **Source Data** field of the Data tab and then press the ENTER key. Alternatively, you can click the [Select] button to find and set SAMPSIO.DMAGECR as the input data source.

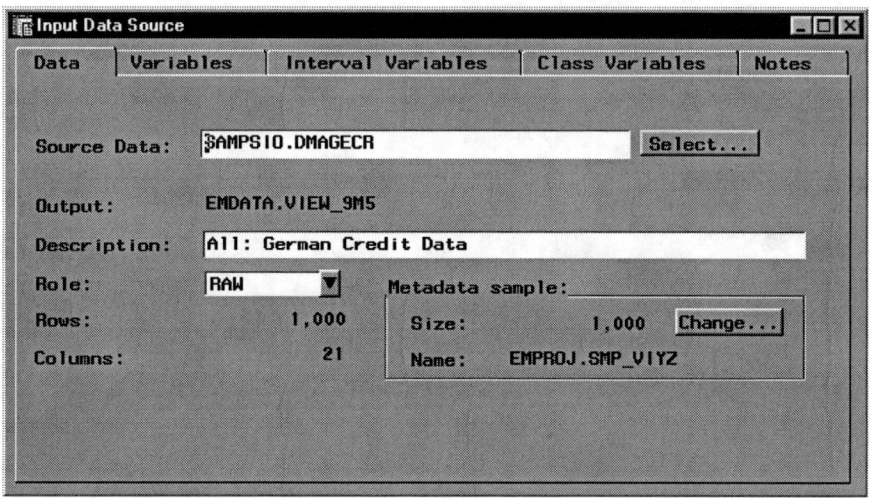

The node automatically creates the metadata sample, which is used in several Enterprise Miner nodes to determine metadata information about the analysis data set. By default, the metadata sample consists of a random sample of 2,000 cases. Because there are only 1,000 customer cases in this data set, the metadata sample contains all the customer cases in the SAMPSIO.DMAGECR data set. Enterprise Miner assigns a model role and measurement level to each variable that is listed in the Variables tab based on the metadata sample. You can reassign the model role or measurement level for a variable. The summary statistics for interval and class variables are also calculated from the metadata sample.

You can control the size of the metadata sample by selecting the [Change] button in the Data tab.

Note: The SAMPSIO.DMAGECR credit data set is small relative to many data marts, which often contain gigabytes or even terabytes of data. Therefore, there is no need to sample this data set with a *Sampling* node prior to creating the partitioned data sets with the *Data Partition* node. △

3. Setting the Target Variable

You must assign the target role to the appropriate variables in the input data source. If you have multiple targets, you can use a *Group Processing* node to generate separate models for each target variable in one run of the process flow diagram. For this example, there is one target variable named GOOD_BAD.

To assign the target model role to GOOD_BAD, follow these steps:

1 Select the Variables tab.

2 Scroll down (or page down) the Input Data Source window to display the variable GOOD_BAD.

3 Right-click in the **Model Role** cell of the row that contains the GOOD_BAD variable and select the **Set Model Role** pop-up menu item. Another pop-up menu opens.

4 Select **target**. Do not close the *Input Data Source* node.

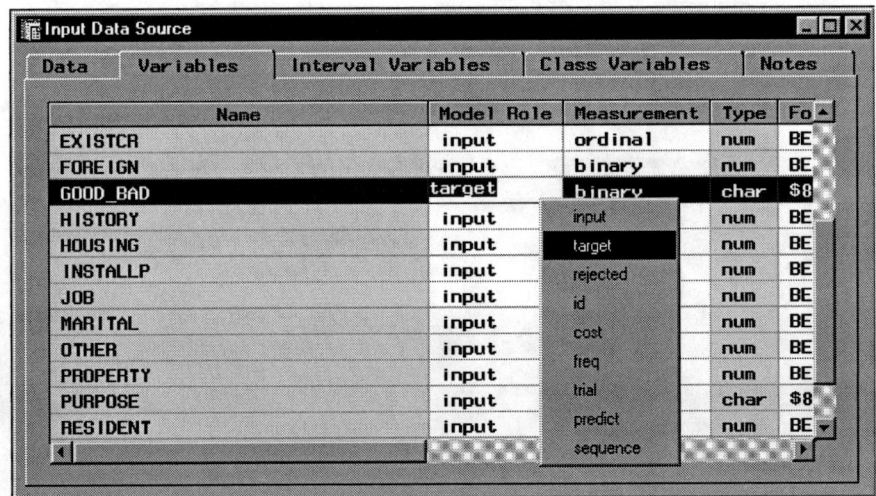

4. Defining a Target Profile for GOOD_BAD

A target profile contains information for the target, such as the event level for binary targets, decision matrices, and prior probabilities. The active target profile information is read downstream in the process flow by the modeling nodes and the *Assessment* node. Although you can define and edit a target profile in any of the modeling nodes, it is often convenient to define this information up front in the process flow when you set the target variable in the *Input Data Source* node.

In this section, you will set the target event level, specify the loss matrix, and define the prior vector for the target GOOD_BAD. Follow these steps to define the target profile for GOOD_BAD:

1 Open the Target Profiler by right-clicking in any cell of the GOOD_BAD target variable row of the Variables tab, and select **Edit target profile**. The Target Profiles for the GOOD_BAD window opens.

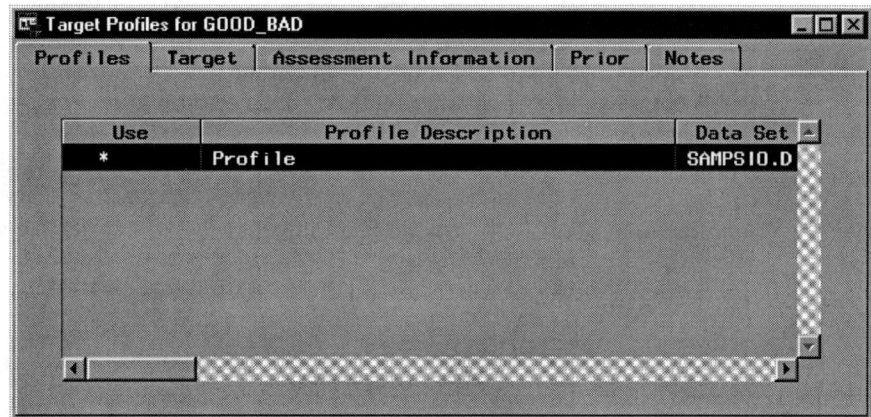

By default, the Target Profiles for the GOOD_BAD window contains a predefined profile. The asterisk beside the profile name indicates that it is the active target profile. You can create new target profiles, but for this example, you will modify the existing profile.

2 Set the Target Event Level:

Select the Target tab. By default, the *Input Data Source* node sets the **Order** value to **Descending** for binary targets. Because the order is set to descending by default, **good** is the target event level. You will model the probability that a customer has good credit. The *Assessment* node is dependent on the event level when calculating assessment statistics, such as expected profit or loss. If you wanted to model the probability that a customer has bad credit, you would need to set the event level to bad. You can accomplish this by setting the **Order** value for GOOD_BAD to **Ascending** in the Class tab of the Input Data Source window.

3 Define the Loss Matrix for the Target GOOD_BAD:

a You use the Assessment Information tab to define decision matrices, and set the assessment objective for each matrix to either maximize profit, maximize profit with costs (revenue), or minimize loss. For binary targets, the Assessment Information tab contains four predefined decision matrices. These matrices cannot be redefined and are not suitable for this example – you want to define the realistic loss matrix that was described in the overview of the process flow.

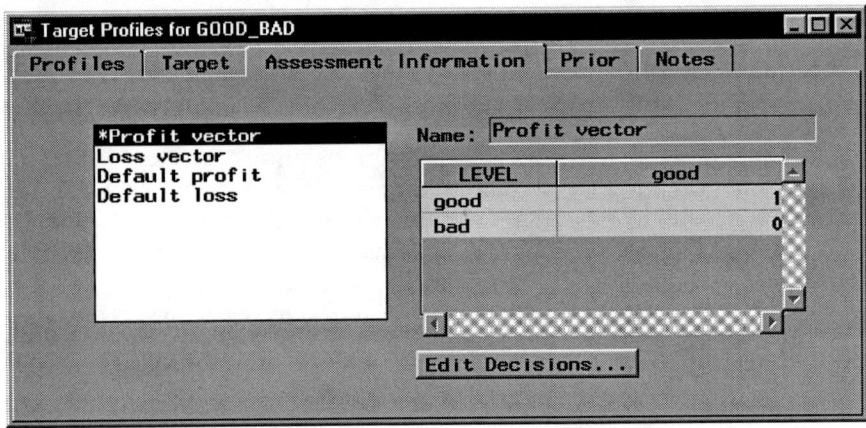

b You can add a new loss matrix that you can modify by copying the **Default Loss** matrix (right-click on the **Default Loss** matrix and then select **Copy**). A new decision matrix named **Profit matrix** is added to the list box. Alternatively, you can add a new decision matrix by right-clicking on an open area of the list box, and selecting **Add**. This matrix will always also be a copy of the **Default profit** matrix.

c Only one matrix can have a status of Use. To set the status of the new matrix to Use, select the **Profit matrix** entry, right-click on the entry, and select the **Set to use** menu item. An asterisk appears besides the matrix name indicating that it is now the active decision matrix that will be read downstream in the process flow by the modeling and *Assessment* nodes.

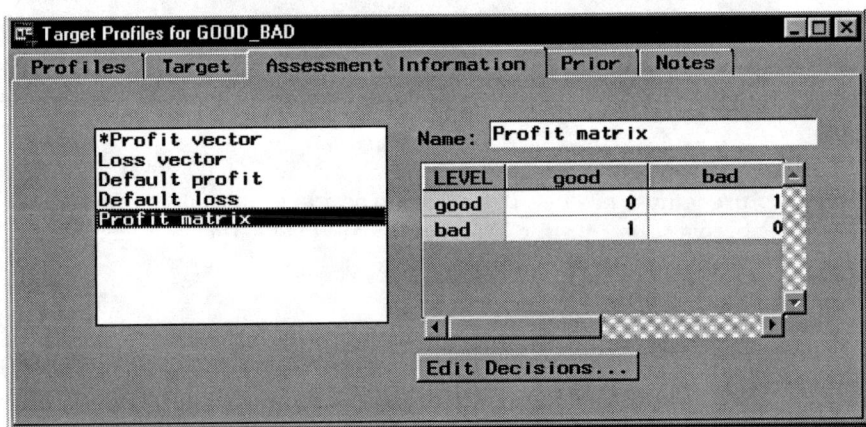

d To rename the matrix, delete the existing name in the **Name** field, type a new name, and then press the ENTER key. In this example, the matrix has been renamed **Realistic Loss**.

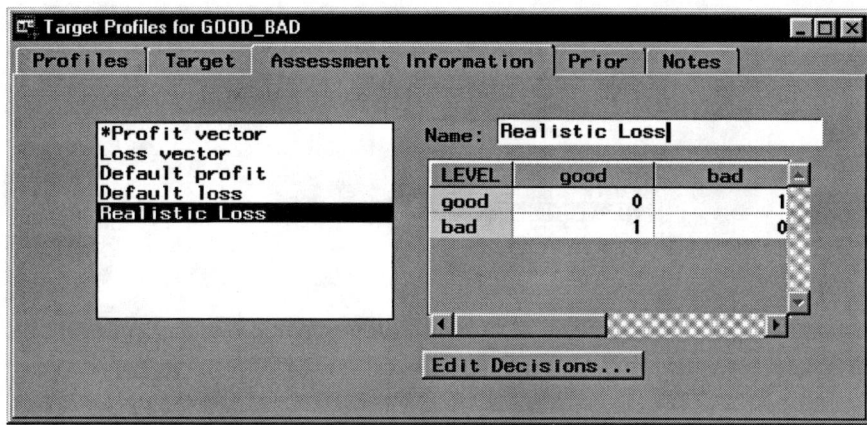

Note: The values in the matrix are still the same as the predefined **Default Loss** matrix that you copied. You use this matrix to obtain the correct misclassification rate for the good and bad credit risk applicants. △

e By default, the decision column names are set to the target levels (good and bad). To rename the decision column names to accept and reject, click Edit Decisions, and then type **accept** in place of the decision named **good**, and type **reject** in place of the decision named **bad**.

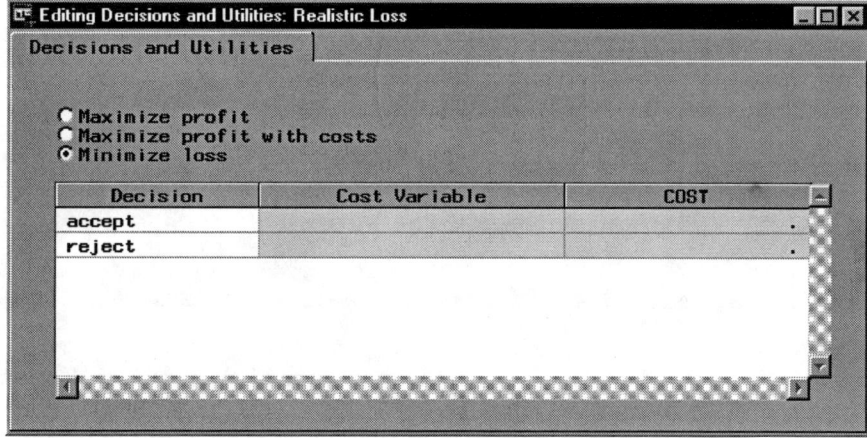

Note: You can also use the Decisions and Utilities tab to set the assessment objective for the matrix to either **Maximize profit**, **Maximize profit with costs** (revenue), or **Minimize loss**. Because you copied the predefined **Default loss** matrix, the assessment objective is already correctly set to **Minimize loss**. If you set the assessment objective to **Maximize profit with costs**, you can assign a cost variable or a constant cost to each decision. To assign a cost variable to a decision, the cost model role must have been assigned to the appropriate variables in the Variables tab of the *Input Data Source* node. △

f Close the Editing Decisions and Utilities window and follow the prompts to save your changes. Click Yes to return to the Assessment Information tab.

g Type the following values in the loss matrix:

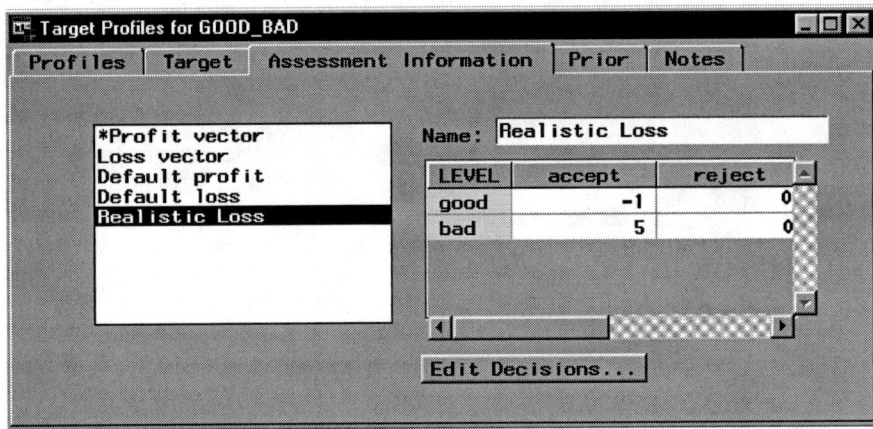

Each of the modeling nodes will use this loss matrix to calculate the expected
losses.

h   To specify the true operational priors for the data that you intend to score,
select the Prior tab.

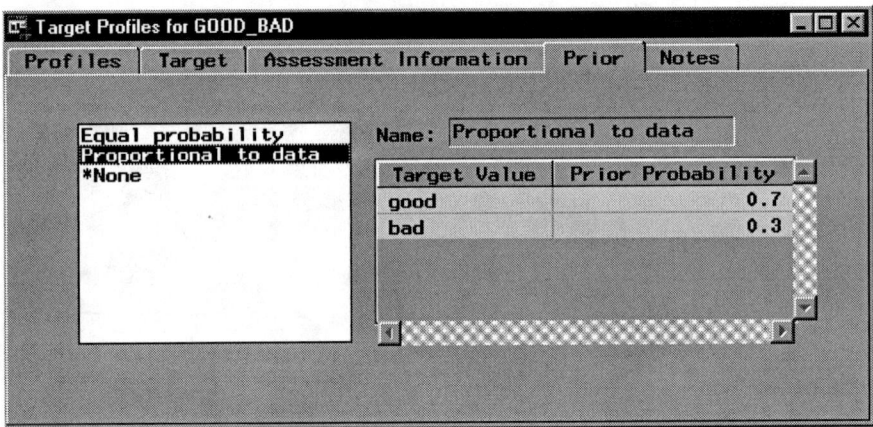

By default, there are three predefined prior vectors. The **Equal probability**
vector contains equal probabilities for the target levels. The **Proportional to
data** vector contains priors that are proportional to those in the input data set.
Note that the input data set contains 70% good risk applicants and 30% bad
risk applicants. The actual probabilities in the score data set are believed to be
90% and 10% for good and bad credit risk applicants, respectively. The active
None prior vector computes the posterior probabilities under the assumption
that the prior probabilities are proportional to the frequencies of the classes in
the training data set.

i   To add a new prior vector, right-click in an open area of the list box and select
the **Add** pop-up menu item. A new **Prior vector** is added that contains prior
values that are also proportional to those in the input data set.

j   To set the status of the vector to use, right-click on the **Prior vector** and
select the **Set to Use** pop-up menu item.

k   Type the following values in the **Prior Probability** cells of the **Prior vector**:

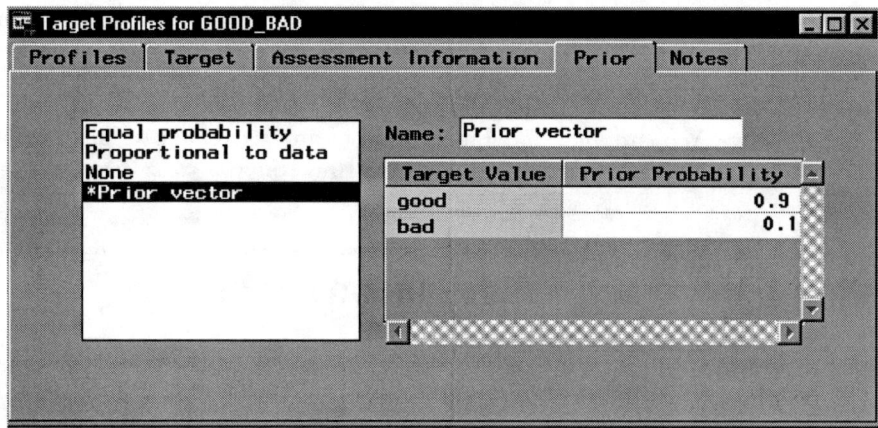

The prior probabilities will be used to adjust the relative contribution of each class when computing the total and average loss.

I Close the window and follow the prompts to save your changes to the target profile. You are returned to the Variables tab of the *Input Data Source* node. Do not close the *Input Data Source* node.

5. Examining Summary Statistics for the Interval and Class Variables

It is advisable to examine the summary statistics for the interval and class variables prior to modeling. Interval variables that are heavily skewed and that have large kurtosis values may need to be filtered and/or transformed prior to modeling. It is also important to identify the class and interval variables that have missing values. The entire customer case is excluded from the regression or neural network analysis when a variable attribute for a customer is missing. Although we tend to collect much information about our customers, missing values are common in most data mining data marts. If there are variables that have missing values, you may want to consider imputing these variables with the *Replacement* node.

1 To view summary statistics for the interval variables, select the Interval Variables tab. The variable AMOUNT has the largest skewness statistic. The skewness statistic is 0 for a symmetric distribution. Note that there are no missing values for the interval variables.

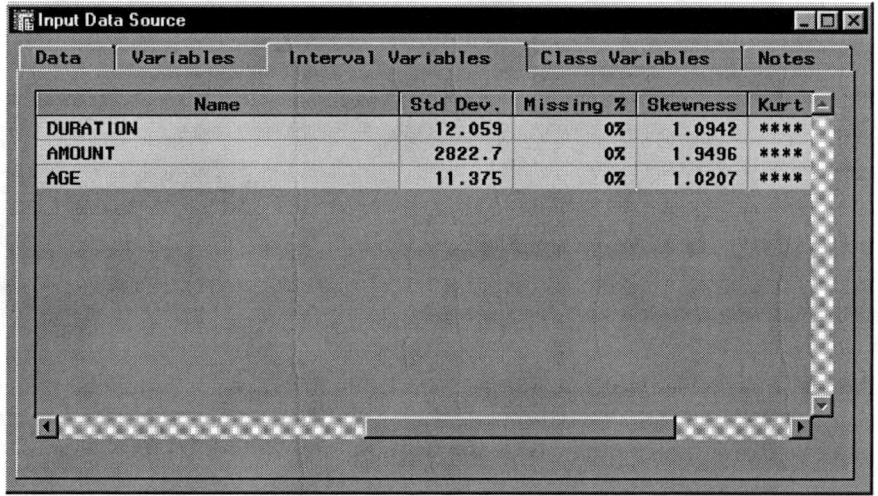

2 To view summary statistics for the class variables, select the Class Variables tab. Note that also there are no missing values for the class variables.

3 Close the *Input Data Source* node and save all changes when prompted.

Note: You can view the distribution of any variable by right-clicking in a cell in the variable row and selecting **View Distribution of <variable name>**. △

---

6. Creating Training and Validation Data Sets

In data mining, one strategy for assessing model generalization is to partition the input data source. A portion of the data, called the training data, is used for model fitting. The rest is held out for empirical validation. The hold-out sample itself is often split into two parts: validation data and test data. The validation data is used to help prevent a modeling node from overfitting the training data (model fine-tuning), and to compare prediction models. The test data set is used for a final assessment of the chosen model.

Because there are only 1,000 customer cases in the input data source, only training and validation data sets will be created. The validation data set will be used to choose the champion model for screening new credit applicants based on the model that minimizes loss. Ideally, you would want to create a test data set to obtain a final, unbiased estimate of the generalization error of each model.

To create the training and validation data sets, follow these steps:

1 Add a *Data Partition* node to the Diagram Workspace.

2 Connect the *Input Data Source* node to the *Data Partition* node. To connect the nodes, hold the left mouse button down on the outer-right edge of the *Input Data Source* node, drag your mouse pointer to the *Data Partition* node (a line appears), and then release the mouse button.

3 Open the *Data Partition* node. When the node opens, the Partition tab is displayed.

4 Allocate 60% of the input data to the training data set and 40% of the input data to the validation data set (type 0 in the **Test** entry field). To replicate the results of this example flow, use the default seed of 12345, which is listed in the **Random Seed** field.

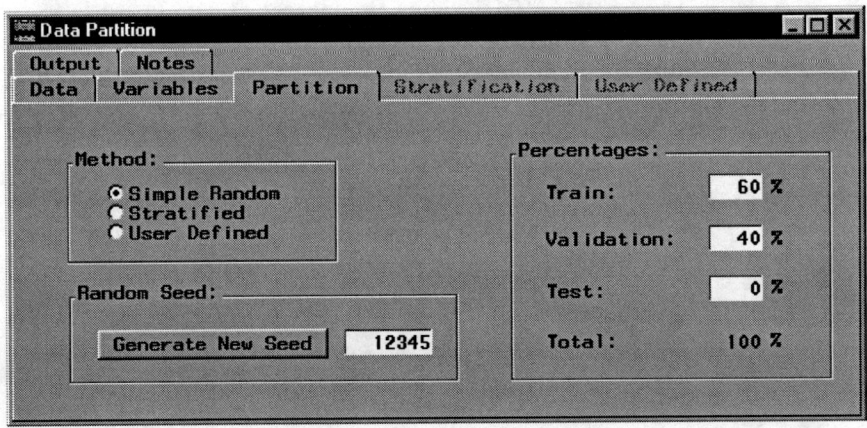

5 Create the partitioned data sets using a stratified sample by the target GOOD_BAD. A stratified sample helps to preserve the initial ratio of good to bad credit applicants in both the training and validation data sets. Stratification is often important when one of the target event levels is rare.

   a Select the **Stratified** method on the Partition tab.
   b Select the Stratification tab.
   c Scroll down to the bottom of the window to display the GOOD_BAD variable.
   d Right-click in the **status** cell of the GOOD_BAD variable row and select the **Set Status** pop-up menu item. Another pop-up menu appears.
   e Select the **use** pop-up menu item.

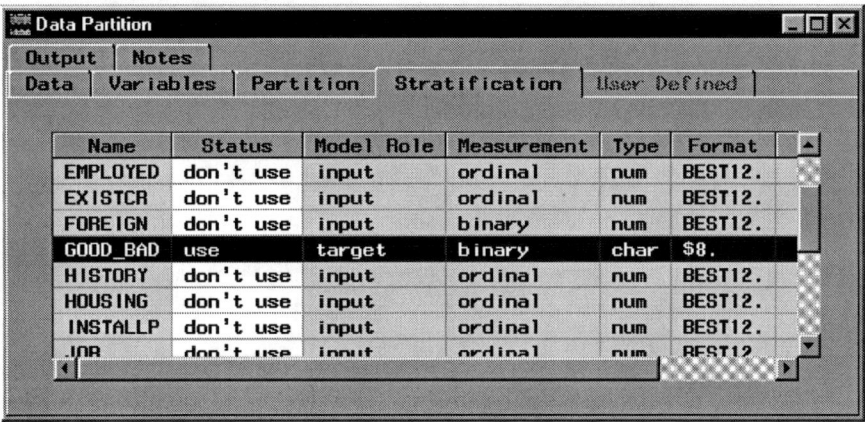

6 Close the *Data Partition* node. Select the Yes button in the Message window to save the node settings.

7. Creating Variable Transformations

Now that you have partitioned the data, you might want to explore the data with exploratory nodes and perhaps modifying the data with modification nodes. For brevity, you will use the *Transform Variables* node to create transformations of existing variables. The data is often useful in its original form, but transformations may help to maximize the information content that you can retrieve. Transformations are useful when you want to improve the fit of a model to the data. For example, transformations can be used to stabilize variance, remove nonlinearity, improve additivity, and correct nonnormality.

1 Add a *Transform Variables* node to the Diagram Workspace.

2 Connect the *Data Partition* node to the *Transform Variables* node.

3 Open the *Transform Variables* node. The Variables tab is displayed.

4 View the distribution of AMOUNT:

   a Right-click in any cell of the AMOUNT variable row and select the **View Distribution of AMOUNT** pop-up menu item. A histogram of AMOUNT is displayed in the Variable Histogram window.

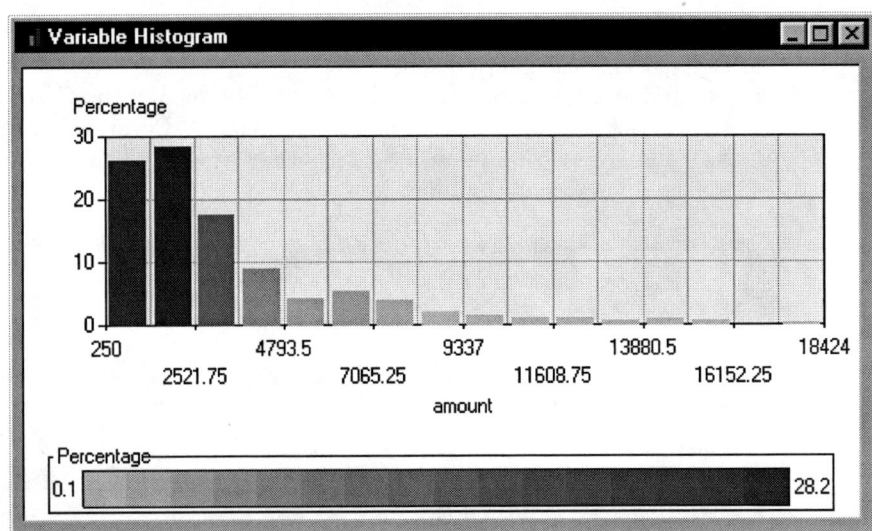

Note: Notice that the distribution for AMOUNT is skewed heavily to the right. The extreme values may cause imprecision in the parameter estimates. △

b   Close the window to return to the Variables tab of the Transform Variables window.

5   Create a new input variable that maximizes the normality of AMOUNT:

a   Right-click in any cell of the row that contains the variable AMOUNT and select the **Transform** pop-up menu item. Another pop-up menu opens.

b   Select the **Maximize Normality** power transformation to create the transformation and return to the Variables tab of the Transform Variables window. **Maximize Normality** chooses the transformation from a set of best power transformations that yields sample quantiles that are closest to the theoretical quantiles of a normal distribution.

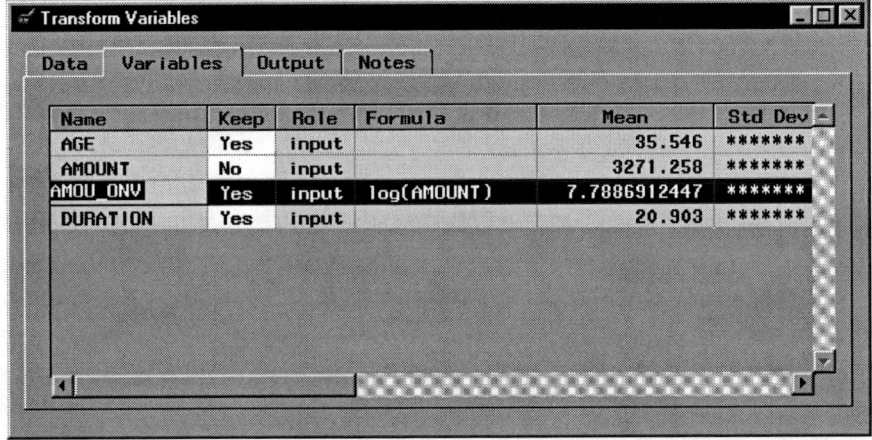

A new variable has been created (for this example, AMOU_ONV), which is the log of AMOUNT. If you scroll to the right, the **Formula** column lists the formula for the transformation. The skewness statistic has been reduced from 1.95 for AMOUNT to 0.13 for the transformed variable AMOU_ONV. The **Keep** status column identifies variables that will be kept and passed to subsequent modeling nodes (**Yes**) and those that will not be (**No**). The keep status for the original input AMOUNT is automatically set to **No** when you apply a transformation.

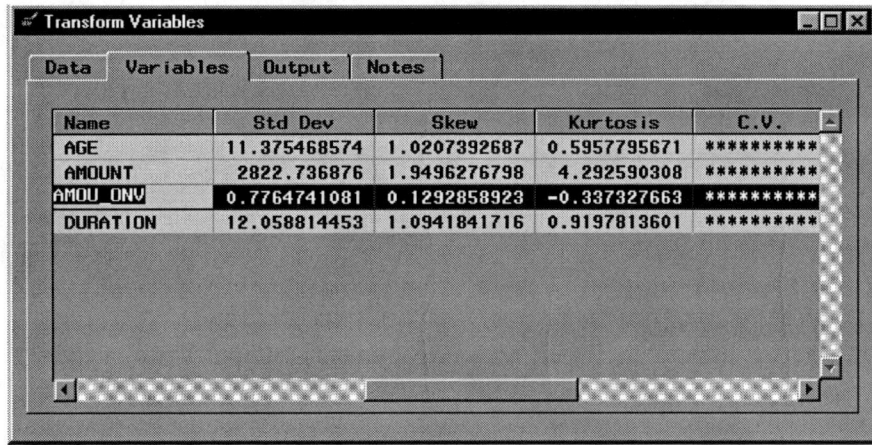

c View the distribution for the log of AMOUNT (for this example, AMOU_ONV).

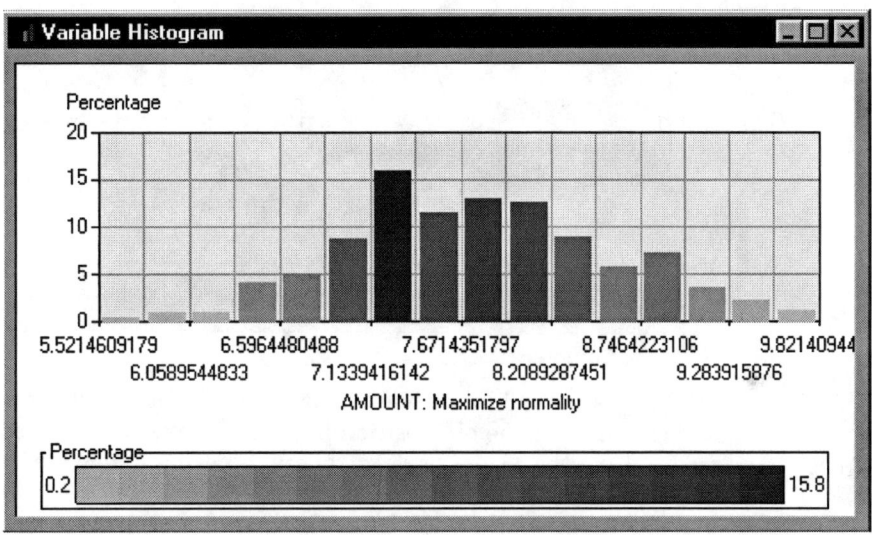

Note: Notice that the distribution for the log of AMOUNT is fairly symmetrical. △

d Close the window to return to the Variables tab of the Transform Variables window.

6 Create an ordinal grouping variable from an interval variable:

With the *Transformation* node, you can easily transform an interval variable into a group variable. Because you are interested in the credit worthiness of particular age groups, create an ordinal grouping variable from the interval input AGE.

a Right-click in any cell of the AGE variable row and select the **Transform** pop-up menu item. Another pop-up menu opens.

b Select **Bucket**. This selection opens the Input Number window, which is used to define the number of buckets (groups) that you want to create. By default, the node creates four buckets.

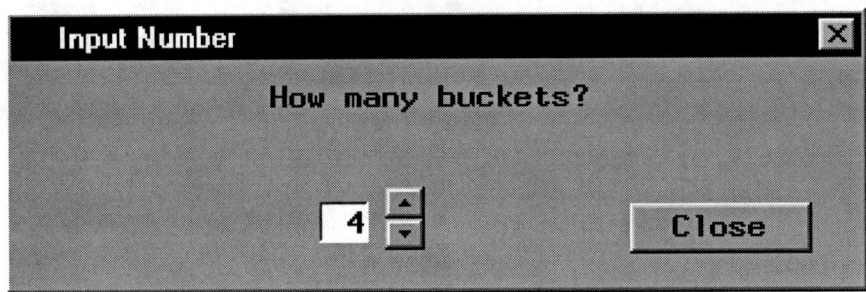

c Select the ⌊Close⌋ button to create the default four buckets. The Select values window opens. It displays the position of each bucket.

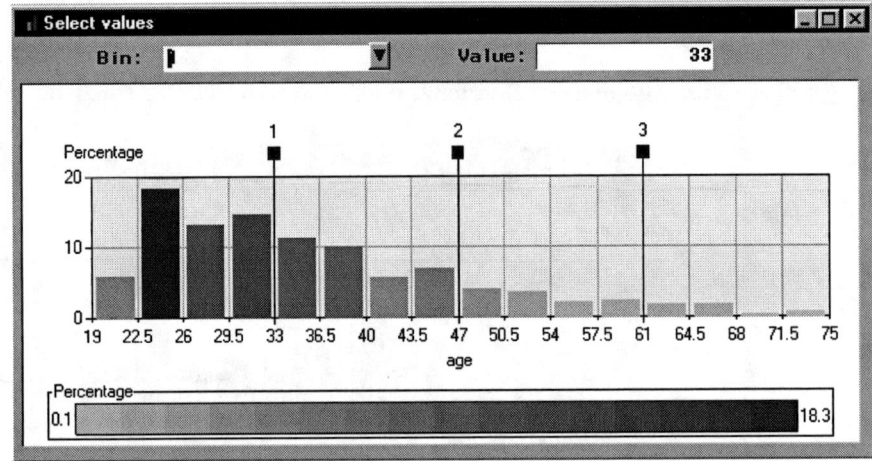

To reposition a bin (bucket), drag the slider bar for the bin to a new location. You can also set the bin position by selecting the bin number that you want to modify from the **Bin** arrow control and entering a new bin value in the **Value** entry field.

d For this example, close the Select Values window to use the default bin positions and to return to the Variables tab. The new bucket variable is added as a variable entry in the Variables tab. The keep status of the original input AGE is set to **No**.

7 Close the *Transform Variables* node. Click the ⌊Yes⌋ button in the Message window to save your changes.

8. Creating a Stepwise Logistic Regression Model

Enterprise Miner enables you to develop predictive models with the *Regression, Neural Network,* and *Tree* nodes. You can also import a model that you developed outside of Enterprise Miner with a *User Defined Model* node, or you can write SAS code in a *SAS Code* node to create a predictive model. Another option is to predetermine the important inputs (reduce the data dimension) with the *Variable Selection* node before modeling with one of the intensive modeling nodes. For more information about predictive modeling, read the Predictive Modeling section in the Enterprise Miner online Nodes help.

Many credit organizations use logistic regression to model a binary target, such as GOOD_BAD. For this reason, a regression model will be the first trained.

1 Add a *Regression* node to the Diagram Workspace.

2 Connect the *Transform Variables* node to the *Regression* node.

3 Open the *Regression* node. The Variables tab lists the input variables and the target. All of the input variables have a status of **use**, indicating they will be used for training. If you know that an input is not important in predicting the target, you may want to set the status of that variable to **don't use** (right-click in the **Status** cell for that input, select **Set Status**, and then select **don't use**). For this example, all variable inputs will be used to train the model.

4 For this example, use a stepwise regression to build the model. Stepwise regression systematically adds and deletes variables from the model based on the **Entry** and **Stay** significance levels (defaults of 0.05). Select the Selection Method tab and then click the **Method** drop-down arrow to select the **Stepwise** item.

5 By default, the *Regression* node chooses the model with the smallest negative log likelihood. For this example, the node should automatically set the **Criteria** field to **Profit/loss**. **Profit/loss** chooses the model that minimizes the expected loss for each decision using the validation data set. Because the validation data set will be used to fine-tune the model and to assess the model, ideally you would want to withhold a test data set to perform an unbiased assessment of the model.

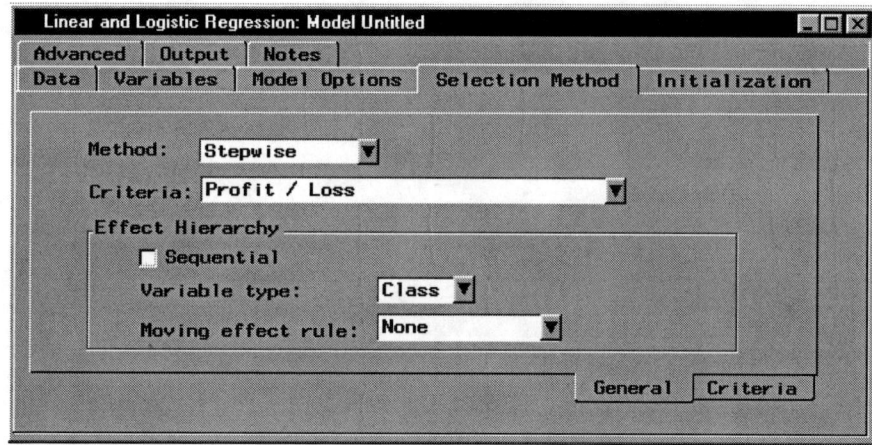

6 Select the Model Option tab. Notice that Type (of regression) is set to **Logistic** in the Regression subtab. If the target was an interval variable, such as average daily balance, then the type would automatically be set to **Linear**.

7 Select the Target Definition subtab of the Model Options tab. Notice that the event level is set to **GOOD**. If you wanted to model the probability of a customer having bad credit, you would need to reset the event level in the target profile. You can edit the target profile by right-clicking on any cell of the target variable row in the Variables tab and selecting the **Edit profile** pop-up menu item.

8 Save the model by using the **File** menu to select **Save Model As**. Type a model name and description in the respective entry fields and then click OK. When you run the node, the model is saved as entry in the Model Manager. By default, the model is named "Untitled."

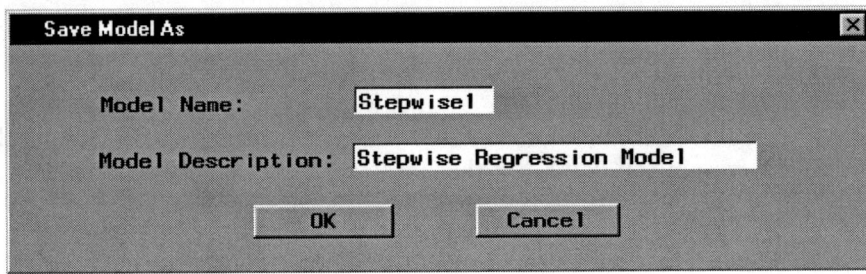

9 Close the *Regression* node.

10 Train the model by right-clicking on the *Regression* node icon in the Diagram Workspace and selecting the **Run** menu item. Because you did not run the predecessor nodes in the process flow, they execute before the *Regression* node begins training. In general, when a node is run, all predecessor nodes need to run in order to pass information through the process flow. You can run the *Regression* node when it is open, but only if you have first run the predecessor nodes in the process flow.

11 Click the Yes button in the Message window to view the results.

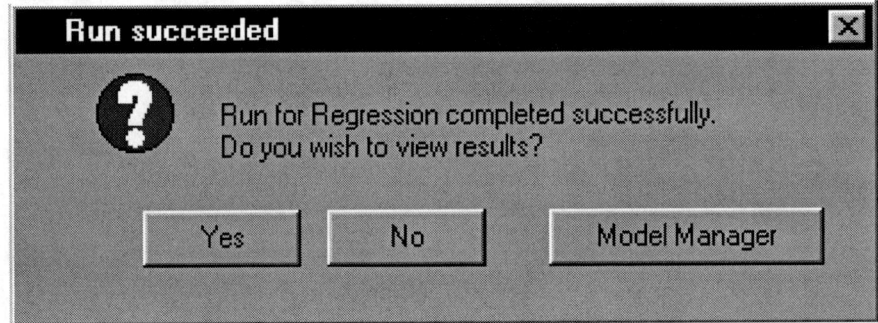

12 When the Regression Results browser opens, the Estimates tab is displayed.

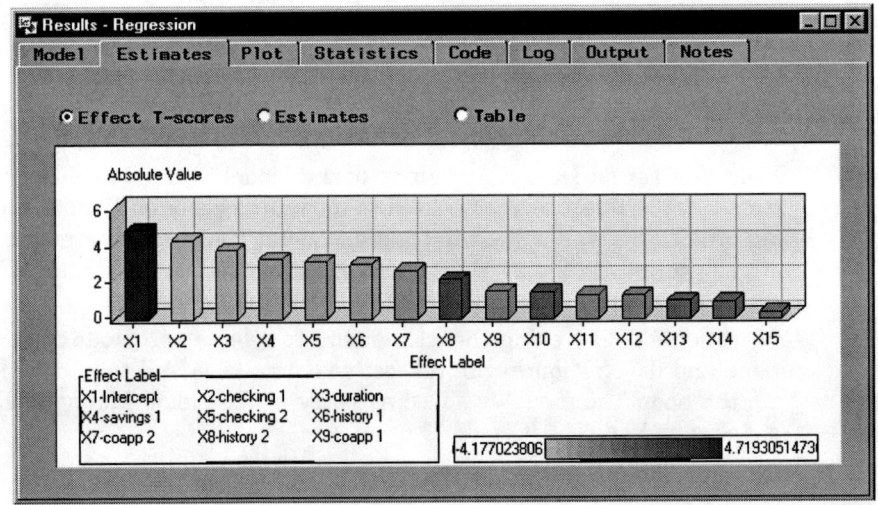

Note: The initial bar chart frame may not have room to display all of the bar effects. To view all of the effect estimates, use the **Format** menu and select **Rescale Axes**. △

The scores are ordered by decreasing value in the chart. The color density legend indicates the size of the score for a bar. The legend also displays the minimum and maximum score to the left and right of the legend, respectively. CHECKING, DURATION, and HISTORY are the most important model predictors.

To display a text box that contains summary statistics for a bar, select the View Info tool

then select and hold mouse button down the bar that you want to investigate.

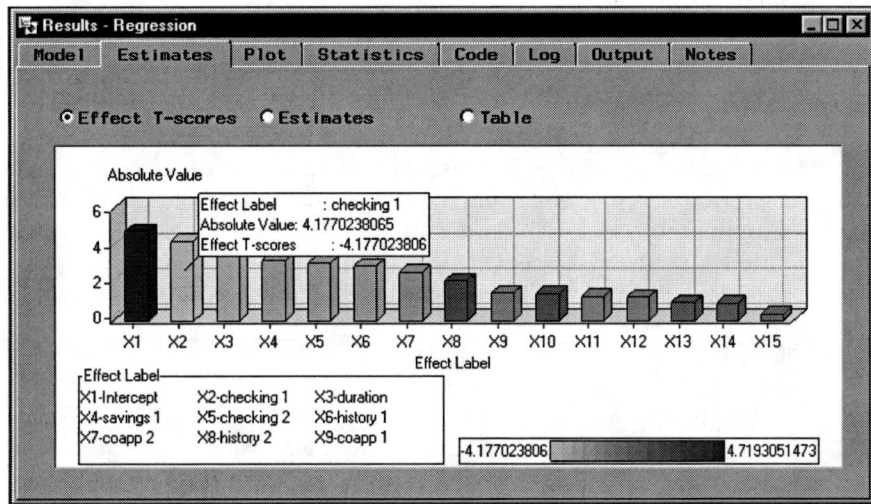

You can use the Move and Resize Legend tool icon on the toolbox to reposition and increase the size of the legend.

To see a chart of the raw parameter estimates, click the **Estimates** radio button to display the parameter estimates plot. An advantage of effect T-scores over the raw parameter estimates is that their size can be compared directly to show the relative strengths of several explanatory variables for the same target. This eliminates the effect of differences in measurement scale for the different explanatory variables.

None of the transformations that you created in the *Transform Variables* node have large absolute effect T-scores. You should work on the exploratory and modification phases of the SEMMA methodology before training models. You can also try different *Regression* node settings to obtain a better fitting model.

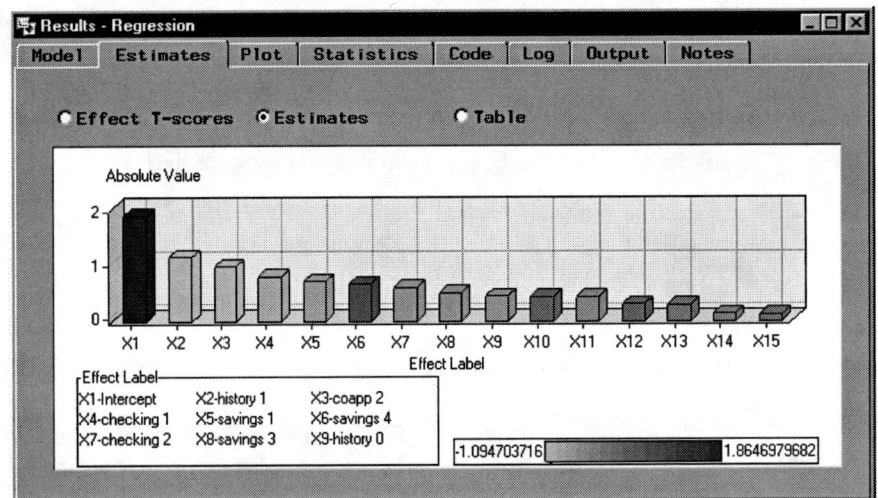

13 Select the Statistics tab to display statistics, such as Akaike's Information Criterion, the average squared error, and the average expected loss for the training and validation data sets. The average loss for the cases in the validation data set is about -54 cents (a 54 cent profit), adjusted for the prior probabilities that you specified in the prior vector of the target profile.

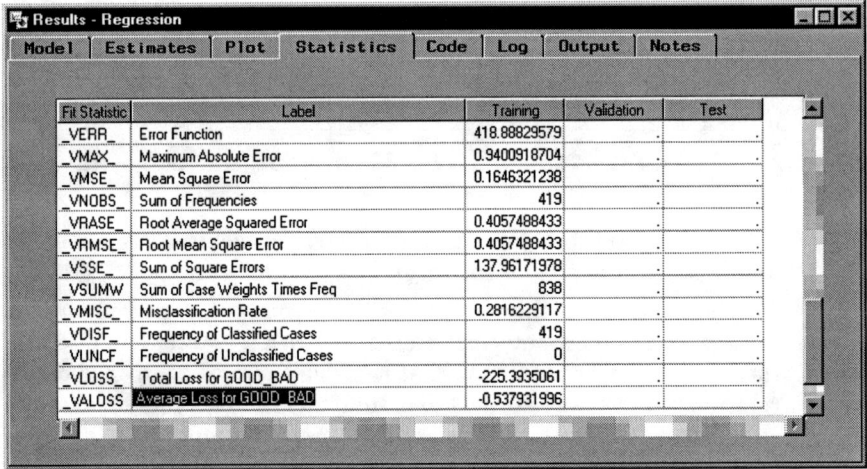

14 Select the Output tab to view the DMREG procedure output. PROC DMREG is the underlying Enterprise Miner procedure that is used to generate the results. The Output tab lists background information about the fitting of the logistic model, a response profile table, and a summary of the stepwise selection process. At each step, odd ratio estimates are provided. Odd ratios are often used to make summary statements about standard logistic regression models. By subtracting one from the odds ratio and multiplying by 100, you can state the percentage in odds for the response for each unit change in a model input. For nominal and binary inputs, odds ratios are presented versus the last level of the input.

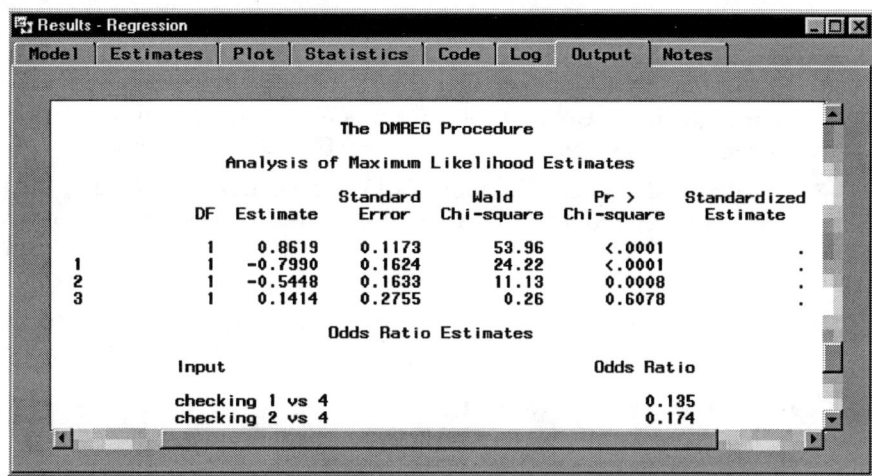

15 Close the Results browser.

9. Creating a Multilayer Perceptron Neural Network Model

The attraction of a standard regression model is its simplicity. Unfortunately, the structure of the standard model does not allow for nonlinear associations between the inputs and the target. If such associations exist, both the predicted response probabilities and any interpretations of the modeling results will be inaccurate.

By adding polynomial and interaction terms to the standard model, nonlinear associations can be incorporated into the logistic regression. To learn more about this task, read the *Regression* node section in the Enterpriser Miner online Nodes Reference help.

Alternatively, you can use another modeling tool such as the *Neural Network* node. The *Neural Network* node enables you to fit nonlinear models like a multilayer perceptron (MLP). Neural networks are flexible classification methods that, when carefully tuned, often provide optimal performance in classification problems such as this one. Unfortunately, it is difficult to assess the importance of individual inputs on the classification. For this reason, MLPs have come to be known as "black box" predictive modeling tools. To create a MLP model:

1 Add a *Neural Network* node to the Diagram Workspace.

2 Connect the *Transform Variables* node to the *Neural Network* node. (Now, both the *Neural Network* node and the *Regression* node are connected to the *Transform Variables* node.)

3 Open the *Neural Network* node. The Variables tab lists the input variables and the target. All of the input variables have a status of **use** indicating that they will be used to train the network. If you know that an input is not important in predicting the target, you might want to set the status of that variable to **don't use** (right-click in the **status** cell for that variable input, and select **Set Status**, and then select **don't use**). For this example, all variable inputs will be used to train the network.

4 The *Neural Network* node provides a basic (default) and an advanced user interface for configuring the network. The basic interface contains a set of easy-to-use templates for configuring the network. The advanced user interface enables you to have more control over configuring the network. For example, you can change the objective function in the advance interface, but not in the basic interface. If you are relatively new to neural networks, you might want to first experiment with different basic network configurations. To configure the network in the advanced interface, you must first select the **Advanced user interface** check box in the General tab. For this example, you will use the advanced interface to see a schematic representation of the network.

5 Because you defined a loss matrix for the GOOD_BAD target, the node automatically sets the model selection criteria to **Profit/Loss**. The node will select the model that minimizes the expected loss for the cases in the validation data set.

6 Select the **Advance user interface** check box. The Advanced tab becomes active and the Basic tab becomes dimmed when you select this check box.

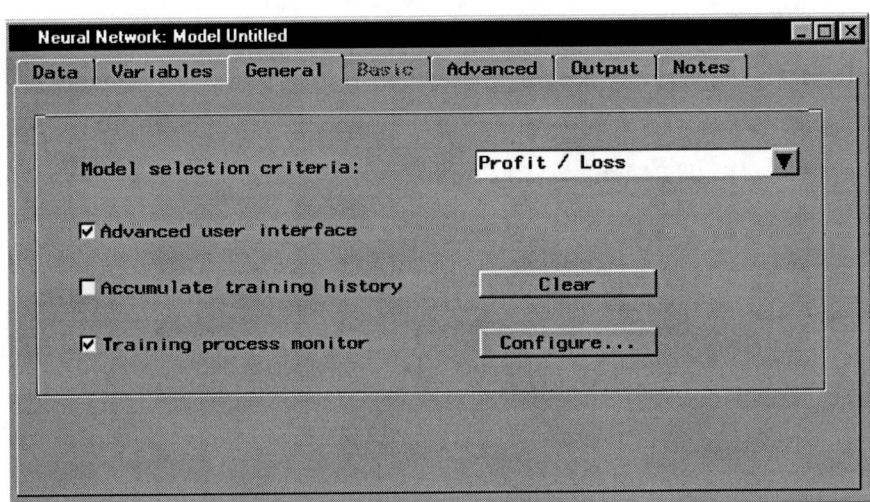

7 To display a schematic representation of the network, select the Advanced tab.

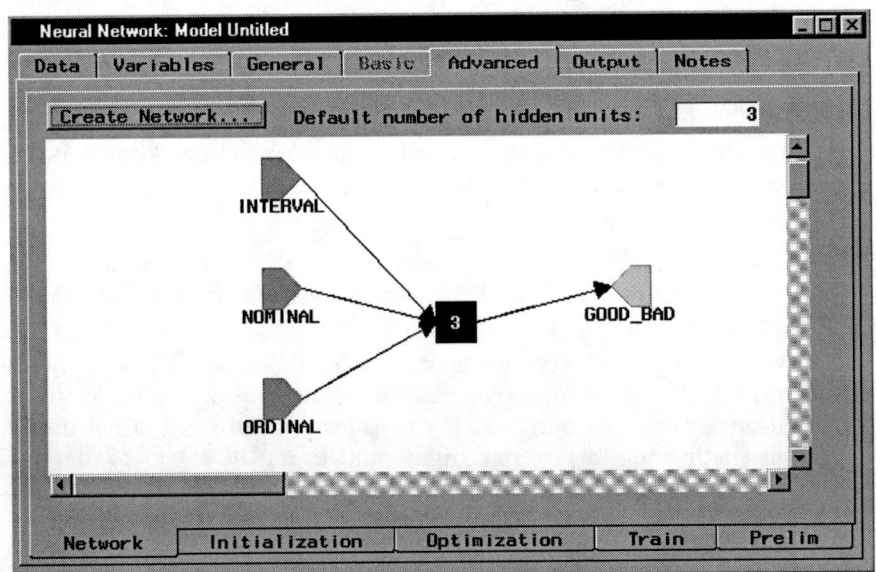

The layer on the left represents the input layer that consists of all the interval, nominal, and ordinal inputs. The middle layer is the hidden layer, which has three hidden units (neurons). The layer on the right is the output layer, which corresponds to the target (GOOD_BAD). When you train the *Neural Network* node, linear combinations of the inputs are transformed by the hidden units and are recombined to form an estimate of the predicted probability of having bad credit.

8 Save the model by using the **File** menu to select **Save New Model**. Type a model name and description in the respective entry fields and then click OK. The model is added as an entry in the Model Manager. By default, the model is saved as "Untitled."

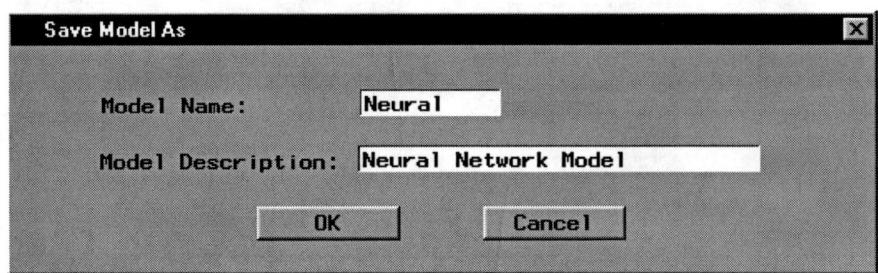

9 Train the model by clicking the Run tool icon at the top of the application.

Note: Because you have already run the predecessor nodes in the process flow, you can run the *Neural Network* node while it is open. △

10 When the node is running, the Neural Network Monitor window displays the error evolution for the training and validation data sets during optimization.

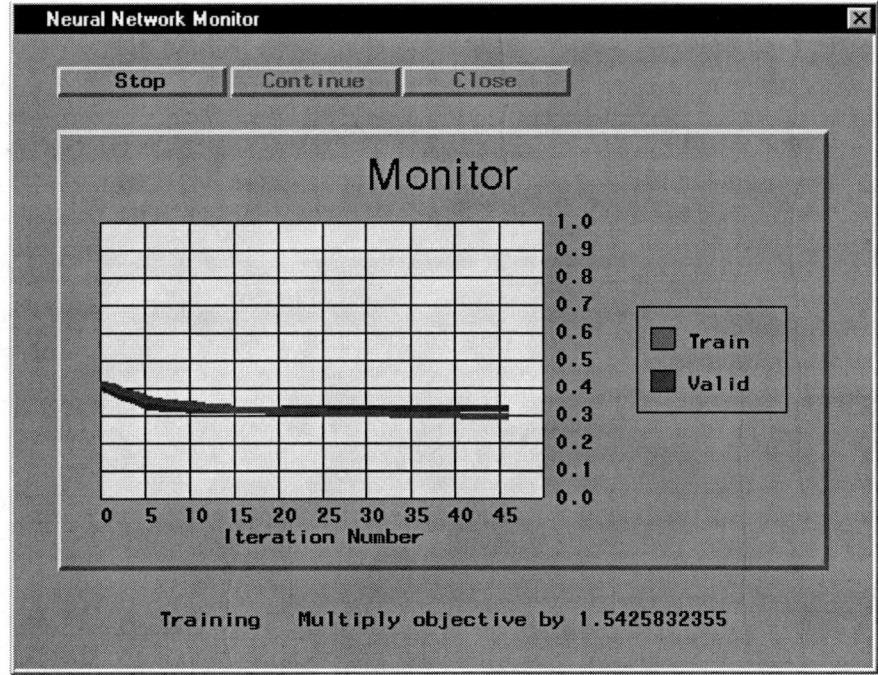

11 After the node finishes training, click the Yes button in the Message window to view the results. By default, the node will complete 100 iterations. You can stop training at any time by clicking the Stop button. Click Continue to continue training. Click Close to stop training altogether and close the monitor.

12 Once the node has completed training, click the Yes button in the Message window to open the results browser.

13 Select the Plot tab of the Results window. By default, the plot shows the average squared error for each iteration of the training and validation data sets.

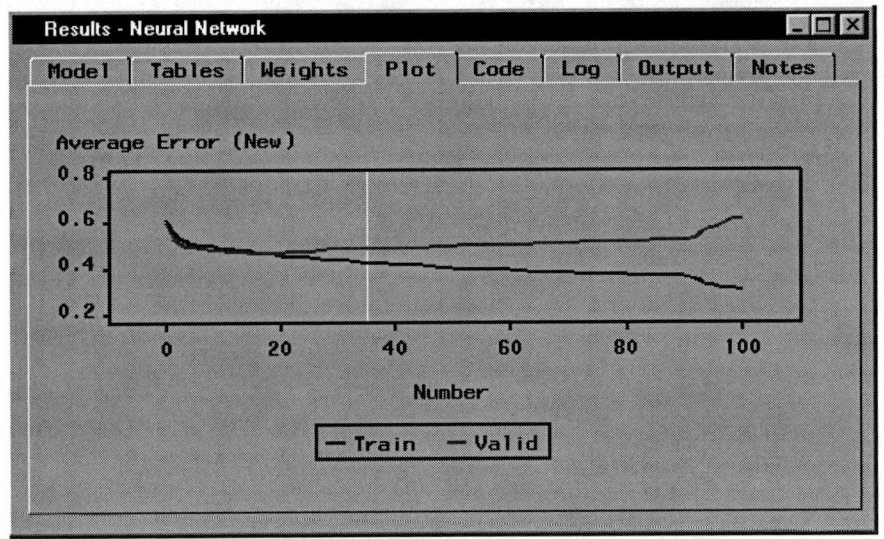

For this example, the optimal average error was achieved at the 35th iteration. Beyond the 35th iteration, overtraining occurs with respect to the validation data set. The network is being trained to the noise in the training data set instead of the underlying patterns in the data. Note how the training and validation lines diverge beyond the 35th iteration. The message indicator panel at the bottom of the window lists the optimal run, step, iteration, and the average square error for the training and validation data sets.

Each time that you open the *Neural Network* node, a new random seed is created and used to generate starting values for training the network. Therefore, your results may differ slightly from the results that are displayed in this document.

14 To view the average loss for each iteration, right-click on the plot and select **Loss**.

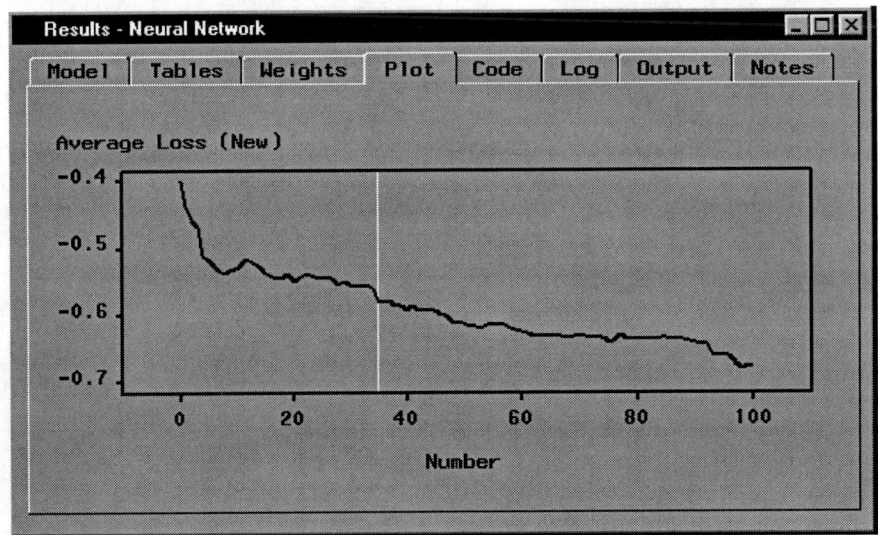

The average expected loss is minimized at the 35th iteration. To access a dialog box that displays the average loss for this iteration, right-click on the plot, select the **Enable pop-up info** item, and then select the vertical, white reference line.

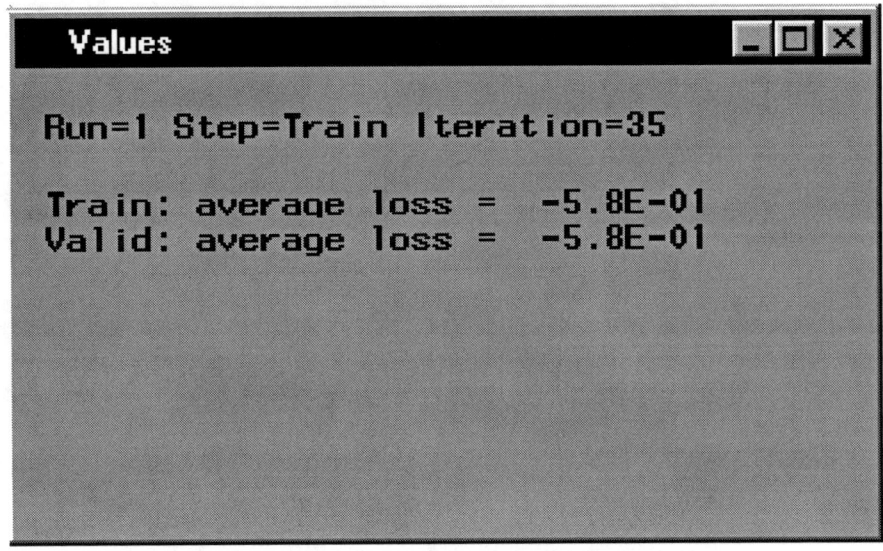

The average profit for the cases in the validation data set is 58 cents. Note that the expected loss of -58 cents is adjusted for the prior probabilities that you specified in the prior vector of the target profile for GOOD_BAD.

15 Close the *Neural Network* Results browser and the *Neural Network* node.

---

10. Creating a Tree Model

An empirical tree represents segmentation of the data created by applying a series of simple rules. Each rule assigns an observation to a segment based on the value of one input. One rule is applied after another rule, resulting in a hierarchy of segments within segments. The hierarchy is called a tree, and each segment is called a node. The original segment contains the entire data set and is called the root node of the tree. A node and all its successors form a branch of the node that created it. The final nodes are called leaves. For each leaf, a decision is made and applied to all observations in the leaf. The type of decision depends on the context. In predictive modeling, as in this example, the decision is simply the predicted value.

Tree models readily accommodate nonlinear associations between the input variables and the target. They offer easy interpretability, and they handle missing values without using imputation.

1 Add a *Tree* node to the Diagram Workspace.

2 Connect the *Transform Variables* node to the *Tree* node.

3 Open the *Tree* node. For binary targets, the node uses a chi-square test with a significance level of 0.200 as the default splitting criterion for binary targets.

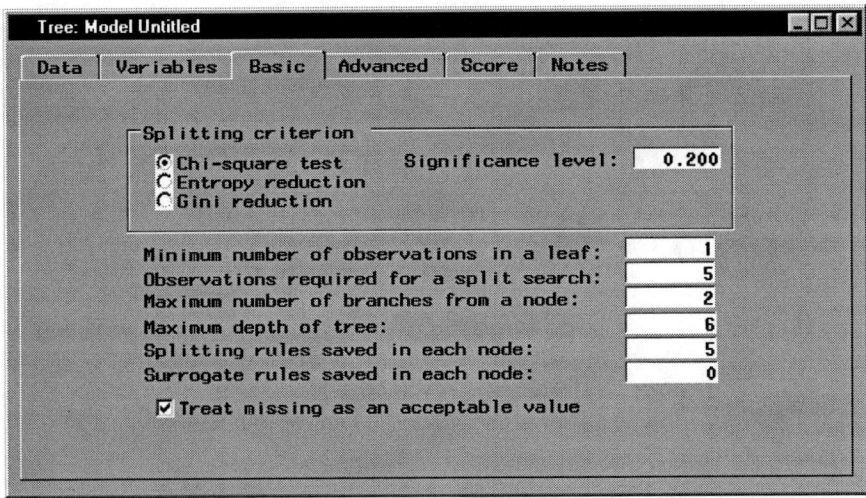

For brevity, use the default Basic tab settings of the *Tree* node to fit the model.

4 Select the Advanced tab. Because the node automatically recognizes that an active loss matrix has been defined, it automatically sets the model assessment measure to **Average Loss**. The best tree will be created based on minimizing the expected loss for the cases in the validation data set.

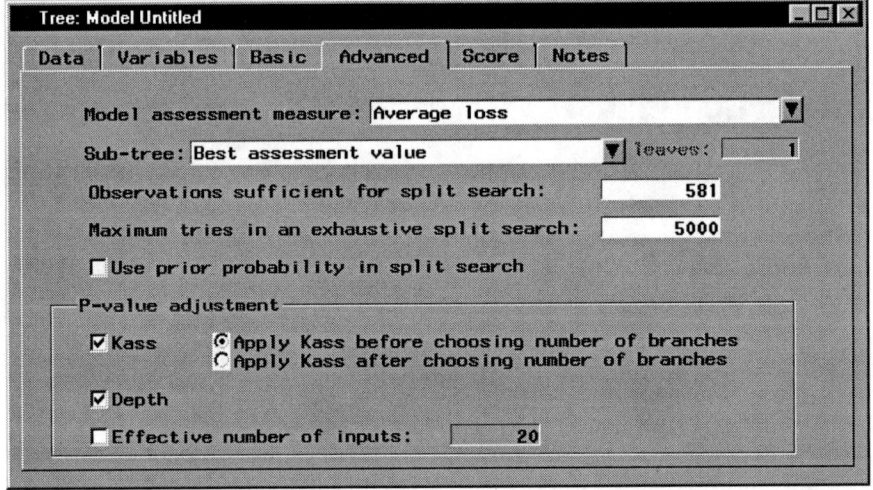

5 Save the model using the **Save** tool icon from the application toolbox. The Save Model As window opens. Type a model name and description in the respective entry fields and then click ⎡OK⎤. By default, the model is saved as "Untitled."

6 Train the node by using the **Run** icon in the application Toolbox.

7 After the node finishes training, click ⎡Yes⎤ in the Message window to view the results.

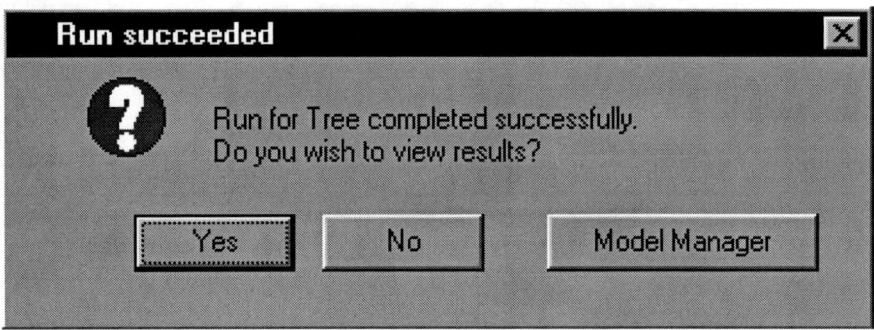

The All tab of the Results browser is displayed:

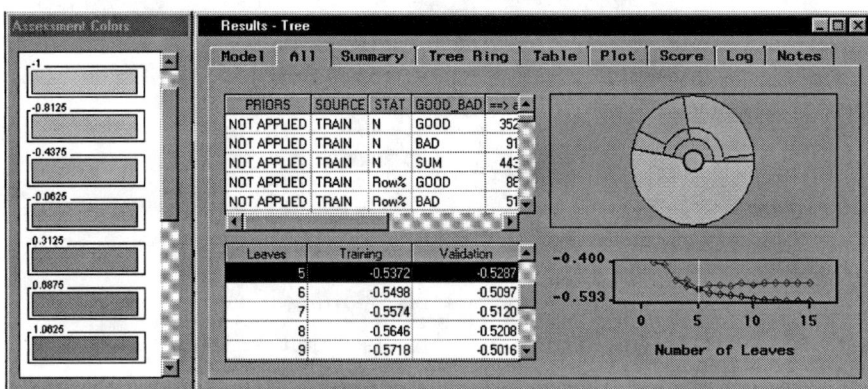

The table in the upper-left corner summarizes the overall classification process. Below this is another table that lists the training and validation expected loss values for increasing tree complexity. The plot at the bottom-right corner represents this same information graphically.

The tree with only two leaves provides the smallest expected loss for the validation data. The average expected loss for the cases in the validation data set is about -12 cents (a 12 cent profit).

The tree ring provides a quick overview of the tree complexity, split balance, and discriminatory power. The center of the ring corresponds to the root node of the tree — the farther from the center, the deeper the tree. A split in the ring corresponds to a split in the tree. The arc length of the regions within each ring corresponds to the sample sizes of the nodes. Darker colors represent node purity (these nodes have minimal expected loss values). The Assessment Colors window contains the segment color hues that correspond to the expected loss values in the tree ring.

8 To view the more traditional tree diagram, click the **View** menu and select **Tree**.

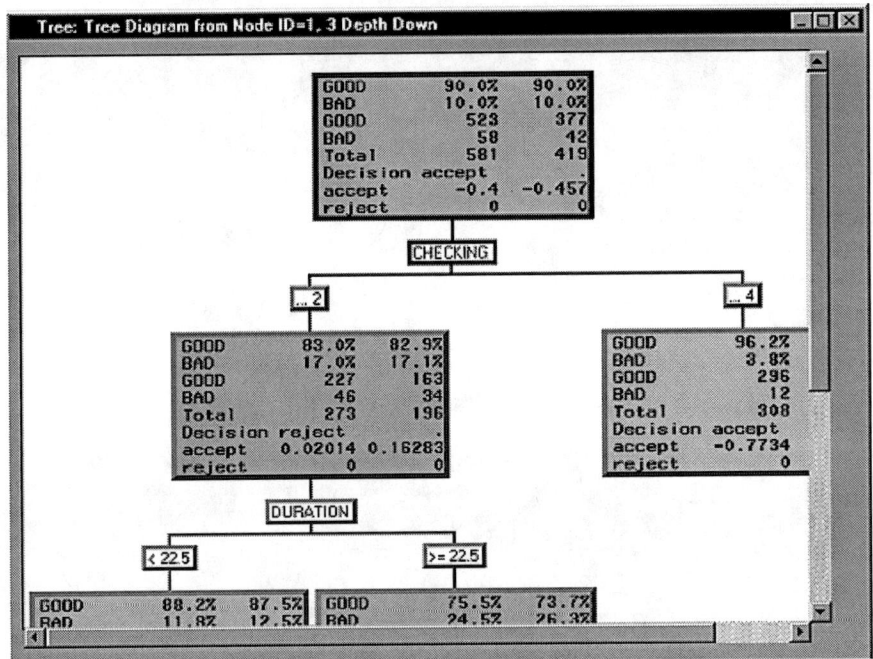

The tree diagram contains the following items:

☐ Root node — top node in the tree that contains all cases.

☐ Internal nodes — nonterminal nodes (also includes the root node) that contain the splitting rule.

☐ Leaf nodes — terminal nodes that contain the final classification for a set of observations.

You can use the scroll bars to display additional nodes. The expected loss values are used to recursively partition the data in homogeneous groups. The method is recursive because each subgroup results from splitting a subgroup from a previous split.

The numeric labels directly above each node indicate at which point the *Tree* node found significant splits. The character labels that are positioned central to each split are the variable names. For the credit data, the only input variable that resulted in a split was CHECKING.

When you use the loss assessment criterion to build the tree, each row of a node contains the following statistics:

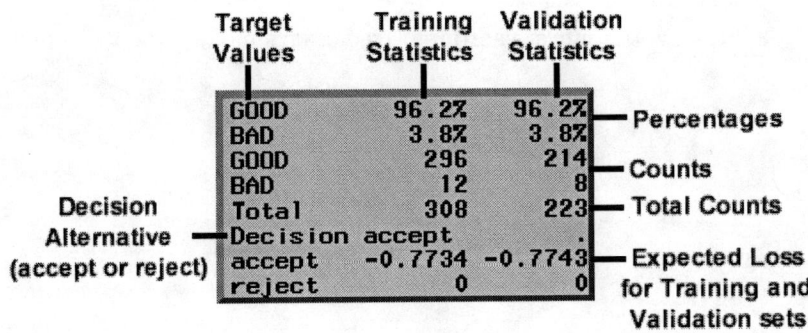

- □ The first row lists the percentage of good values in the training and validation data sets.
- □ The second row lists the percentage of bad values in the training and validation data sets.
- □ The third row lists the number of good values in the training and validation data sets.
- □ The fourth row lists the number of bad values in the training and validation data sets.
- □ The fifth row lists the total number of observations in the training and validation data sets.
- □ The sixth row lists the decision alternative assigned to the node (accept or reject).
- □ The seventh row lists the expected loss for the accept decision in the training and validation data sets.
- □ The eighth row lists the expected loss for the reject decision in the training and validation data sets.

9 Close the Results browser and then close the *Tree* node.

11. Assessing the Models

The *Assessment* node enables you to judge the generalization properties of each predictive model based on their predictive power, lift, sensitivity, profit or loss, and so on.

1 Add an *Assessment* node to the Diagram Workspace.

2 Connect each modeling node to the *Assessment* node. Assessment statistics are automatically calculated by each modeling node during training. The *Assessment* node assembles these statistics, which enables you to compare the models with assessment charts.

3 Open the *Assessment* node. The Models tab of the Assessment Tool window is displayed.

4 Select all three models by dragging your mouse pointer across each model row entry.

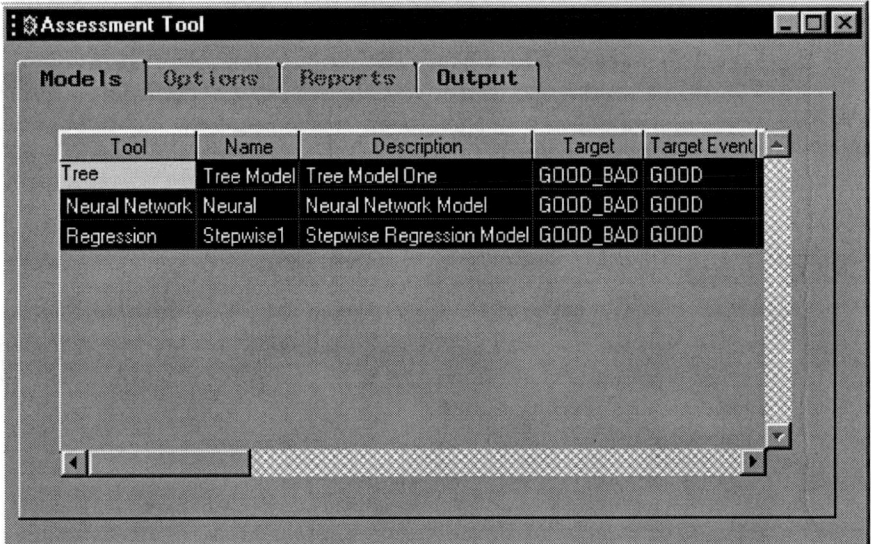

5 To create a lift chart (gains chart) for the models, use the **Tools** pull-down menu to select the **Lift Chart** item. Alternatively, you can create a lift chart by selecting the Draw Lift Chart tool (the second tool on the Toolbox). By default, the validation data set is used to create the assessment charts. For a binary target, the lift chart does not adjust for the expected loss, it only considers the event posterior probabilities.

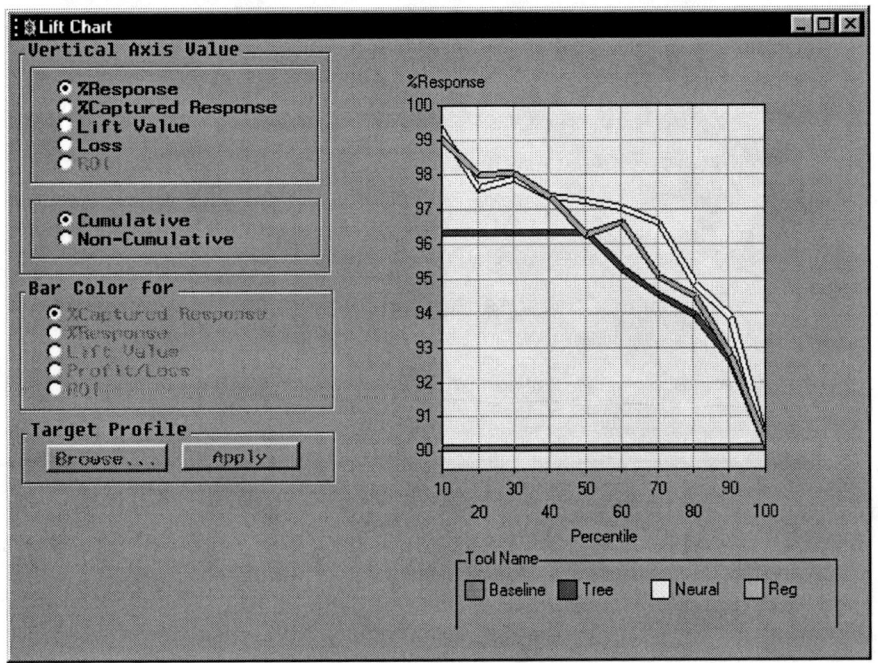

By default, the *Assessment* node displays a cumulative **%Response** lift chart. For this chart, the customer cases are sorted from left to right by individuals most likely to have good credit as predicted by each model. The sorted group is then lumped into ten deciles along the X axis. The left-most decile is the 10% of the customers most likely to have good credit. The vertical axis represents the actual cumulative response rate in each decile.

The lift chart displays the cumulative % response values for a baseline model and for the three predictive models. The legend at the bottom of the display corresponds to each of the models in the chart. The default legend may not have enough room to display all models.

To resize the legend, select the Move/Resize Legend tool icon, click and hold the mouse mouse pointer on the legend resize handles, and then drag the legend to obtain the desired size.

You measure the performance of each model by determining how well the models capture the good credit risk applicants across the various deciles. To display a text box that shows the % response for a point, select the View Info tool, then click and hold on a point.

For the regression model, the second decile contains 97.92% good credit risk applicants.

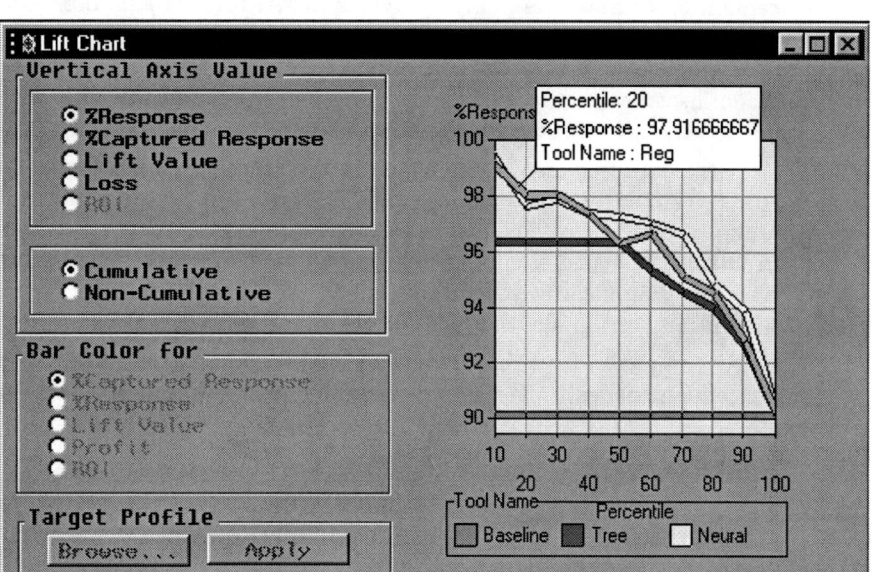

The regression model captures a few more good applicants in the second decile than the neural network model. For the other deciles, the performance of the neural network model is as good as or better than the regression model.

For this data, the tree model does not perform quite as well as the regression and neural network models. Note that since a different random seed is used to generate the starting values for training the neural network, your results may differ slightly from the neural network results displayed in this lift chart.

6 To create a loss chart, select the **Loss** radio button.

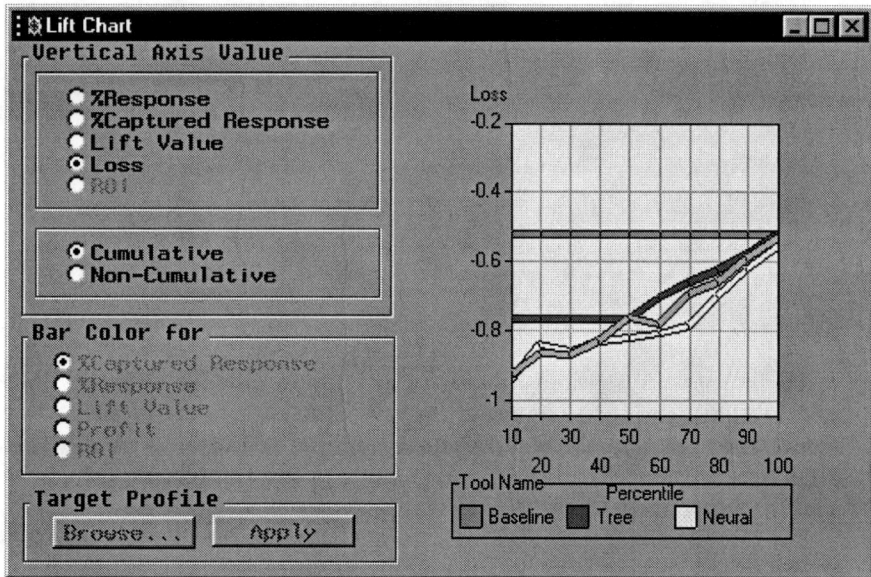

The loss chart shows the expected loss across all deciles for each model and for the baseline model. In the first and second deciles, the regression model provides minimal expected loss values of about -70 and -64 cents, respectively (remember that you can use the View Info tool to probe a point on the loss chart). In the remaining deciles, the neural network model provides smaller expected loss values than does the regression model. The performance of the tree model is not as good as the neural model or the regression model in the earlier deciles. The regression model becomes the poorest performing model beyond the fifth decile. In fact, beyond the seventh decile, the regression model yields positive loss values.

There does not seem to be a clear-cut champion model to use for subsequent scoring. Actually, the German credit data set is a highly random data set, which makes it difficult to develop a really good model. This is typical of data mining problems. The selection of the champion model for scoring ultimately depends on how many applicants you intend to target. For this example, you will use the neural network model to score the SAMPSIO.DMAGESCR data set.

7 Select the model for subsequent scoring. To export the neural network model to subsequent nodes in the process flow (for example, to the *Score* node), follow these steps:

 a Select the Output tab.
 b Click on the Neural Network entry in the **Highlight Model for Output** list box.

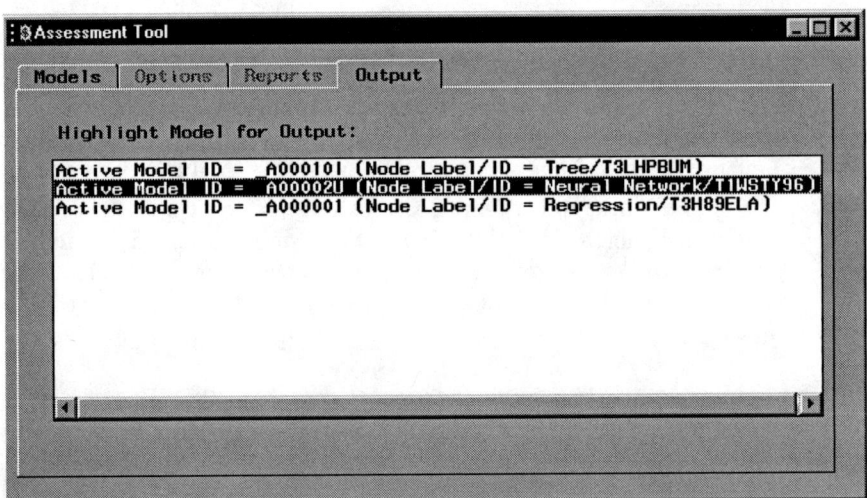

8 Close the *Assessment* node.

12. Defining the Score Data Set

The purpose of predictive modeling is to apply the model to new data. If you are satisfied with the performance of the neural network model, then you can use this model to screen (score) the credit applicants. If you are not satisfied with this model, cycle back through the desired components of the sample, explore, modify, model, and assess methodology to try to obtain a better predictive model.

For this example, SAMPSIO.DMAGESCR is the name of the score data set. It is also stored in the sample library.

Follow these steps to set SAMPSIO.DMAGESCR as the score data set:

1 Add a second *Input Data Source* node to the data mining workspace.

2 Open the *Input Data Source* node.

3 Click the down arrow beside the **Role** item and select Score.

4 Type SAMPSIO.DMAGESCR in the **Source Data** field and press the ENTER key.

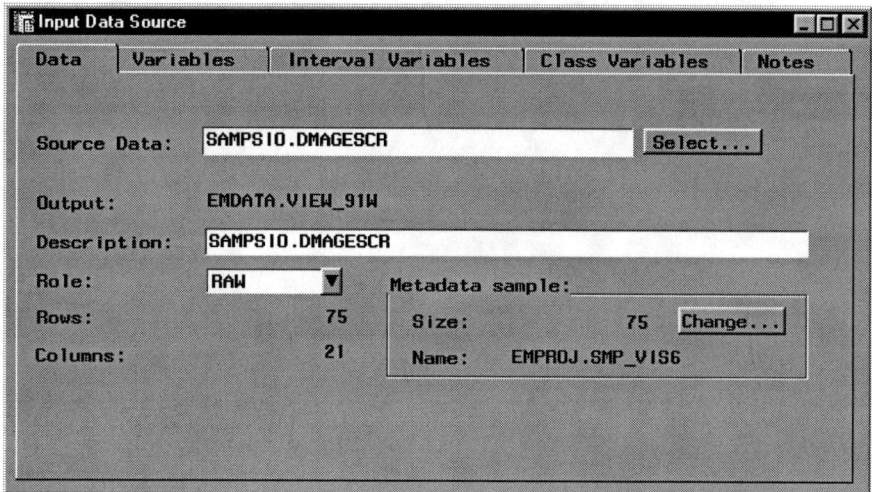

5 Select the Variables tab. Notice that there is not a target variable named GOOD_BAD in this data set. You want to estimate the expected loss for the applicants by applying the scoring formula from the neural network model to this data set.

6 Close the *Input Data Source* node and save changes.

13. Scoring the Score Data Set

The *Score* node generates and manages scoring code that is generated by the nodes in the process flow diagram. The code is encapsulated in the form of a single SAS DATA step, which can be used in most SAS environments even without the presence of Enterprise Miner.

1 Connect the *Assessment* node to the *Score* node.

2 Connect the *Input Data Source* node that contains the score data set to the *Score* node.

3 Open the *Score* node. The Settings tab is displayed. Set the action to **Apply training data score code to score data set**.

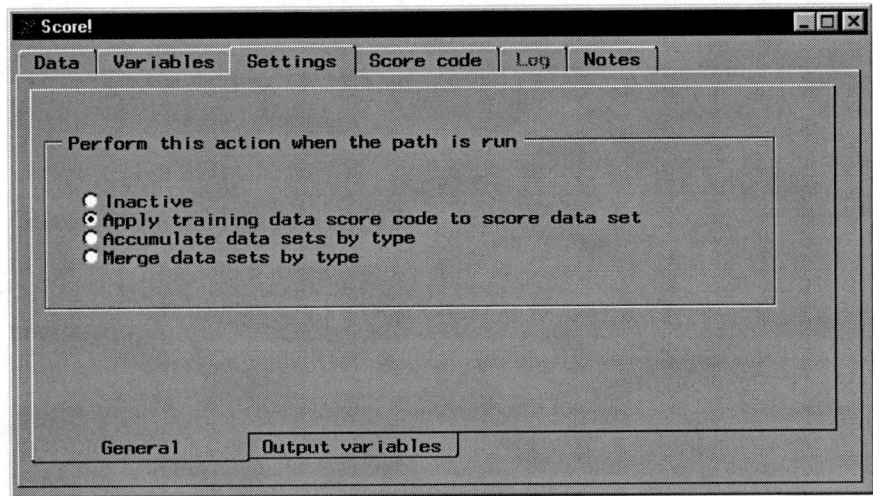

4 Select the Score Code tab to see the current imports. Because you explicitly selected the neural network model in the Output tab of the *Assessment* node, the **Assessment** import contains the scoring code for the neural network model. To view the scoring code, double-click on the **Assessment** current import entry. The code is displayed in the list box to the right.

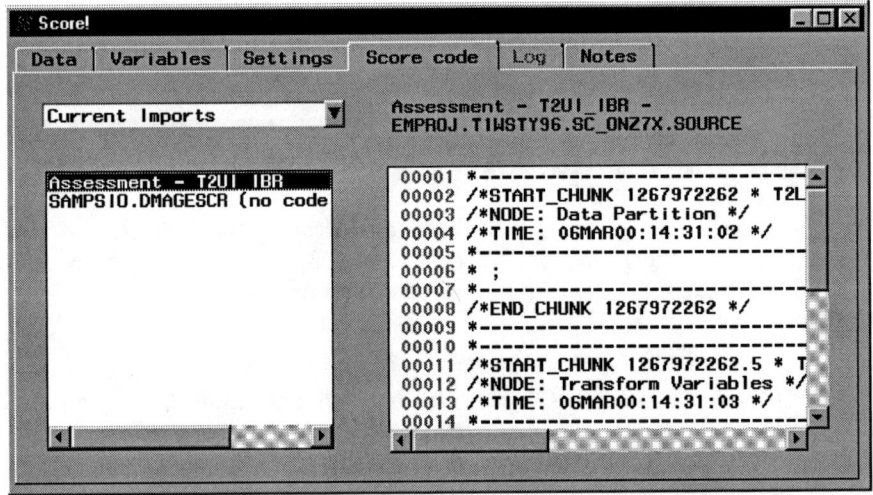

Note: The score data is often much larger than the data from this example, making it more difficult to score within Enterprise Miner. For this reason, many companies often store the score data set (applicant database) on a mainframe computer. You could save and transport this scoring formula to the target mainframe and score the applicant database on the more powerful mainframe. The code contains the entire instructions for scoring. Only base SAS software is required to deploy the code. △

5 Close the *Score* node. Click [Yes] in the Message window to save your changes.

6 To score the SAMPSIO.DMAGESCR data set, right-click on the node icon and then select **Run**. When scoring is completed, click the [Yes] button in the Message window.

14. Viewing the Expected Losses in the Score Data Set

1 Add a *Distribution Explorer* node to the Diagram Workspace.

2 Connect the *Score* node to the *Distribution Explorer* node.

3 Open the *Distribution Explorer* node and select the Data tab. The *Score* node exports the training, validation, and score data sets to the *Distribution Explorer* node. By default, the *Distribution Explorer* node selects the training data set as the active data set. To view the distribution of the expected loss values, you must first set the score data set as the active data set. In the Data tab, click [Select], and then find and select the score data set in the Imports Map window. The score data set name contains the prefix "SD_". Click [OK].

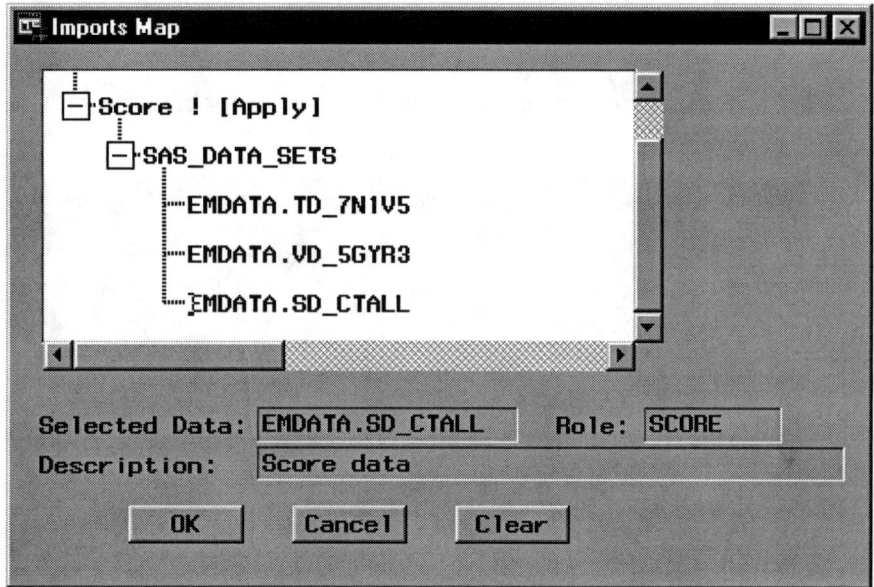

4 Select the Variables tab. When you scored SAMPSIO.DMAGESCR, Enterprise Miner automatically created several score variables, such as predicted values, residuals, and classifications. Two important variables that you will plot are

   □ EL_GOOD_BAD_ — contains the expected loss values for making the good decision.

   □ D_GOOD_BAD_ — assigns either the accept or reject decision status to an applicant in the score data set.

Note: A complete listing of the variable names that are written to the scored data sets can be found in the Predictive Modeling section in the EM Reference Help, accessed from the main menu. △

| Help | ▶ | EM Reference | ▶ | Predictive Modeling |

5 To assign EL_GOOD_BAD_ as the X-axis variable, right-click in the Axis cell for this variable, select **Set Axis**, and then select **X**. Repeat these steps to assign D_GOOD_BAD_ as the Y-axis variable. You will use the D_GOOD_BAD_ variable in code that you write in the SAS Code node. Write down the name of this variable for future reference.

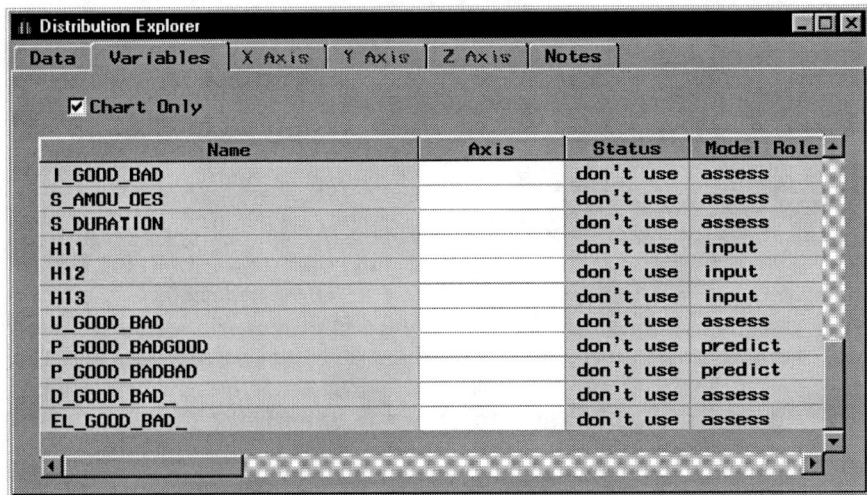

6 To view a histogram of the expected losses for making the good decision, select the X Axis tab.

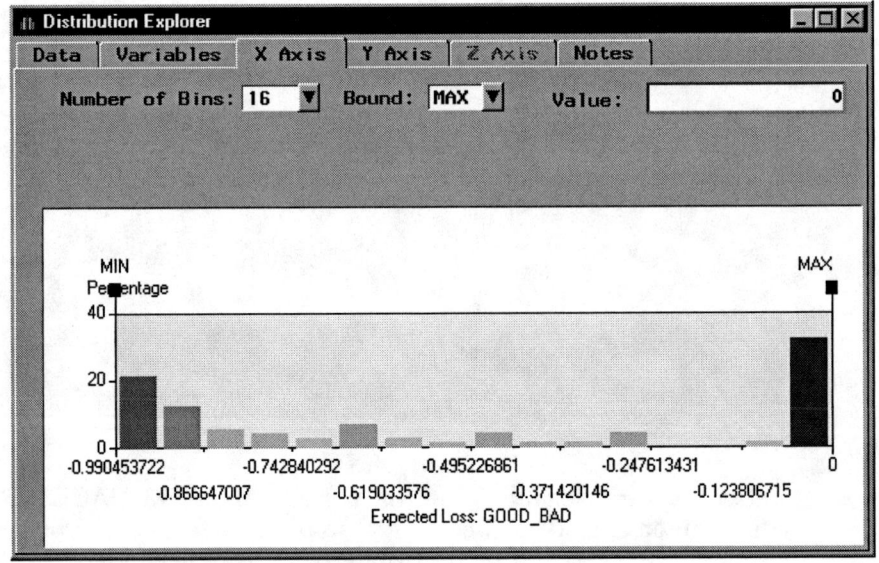

Note: The metadata sample is used to create the histogram in the X axis tab and the bar chart in the Y axis tab. For this example, there are only seventy-five applicants in the score data set. lf the scored data set contains more observations than the metadata sample, then you should examine the histogram that is created when you run the node. The node uses all of the observations in the score data set to generate the graphs shown in the Results browser. △

   Applicants that have negative expected loss values (the yellow bars) represent the customers that pose a good credit risk. All of these customers are assigned to the accept decision (D_GOOD_BAD_=accept). The orange and red bars represent the applicants that pose a bad credit risk. Because these applicants have positive expected loss values, they are assigned to the reject decision (D_GOOD_BAD_=reject).

7 To view a bar chart of the accepted and rejected customers in the score data set, select the Y Axis tab.

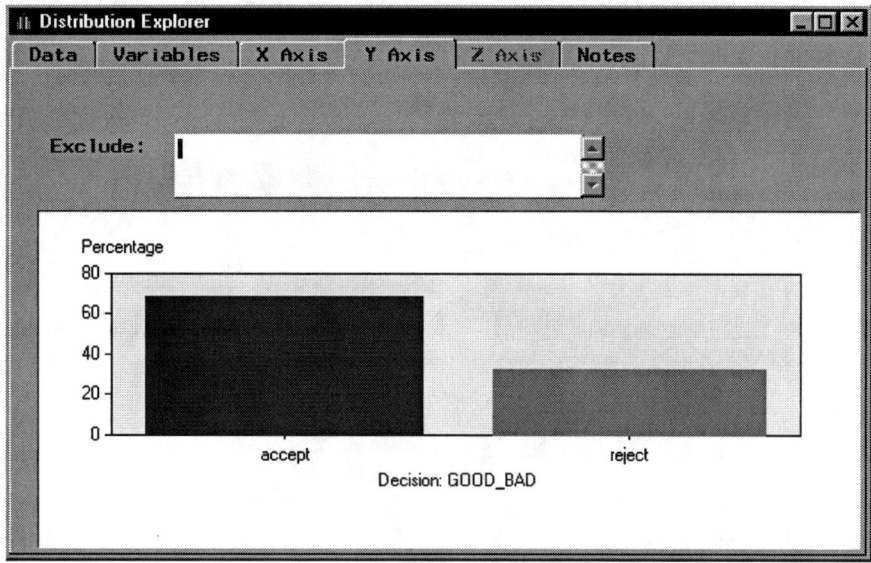

Note: The data in both charts is based on the metadata sample. △

To determine the percentage of accepted and rejected customers in the score data set, use the Probe tool icon and click on a bar: the screen shows that 68% of the applicants were assigned to the accept decision, and 32% of the applicants were assigned to the reject decision.

You can use the *SAS Code* node to create a data set that contains only those customers that pose a good credit risk (accept status). Alternatively, you could use the *Filter Outliers* node to create a data set that contains only the good credit applicants.

8 To create a three-dimensional histogram of the expected losses for the accepted and rejected applicants, use the **Tools** to select **Run Distribution Explorer**.

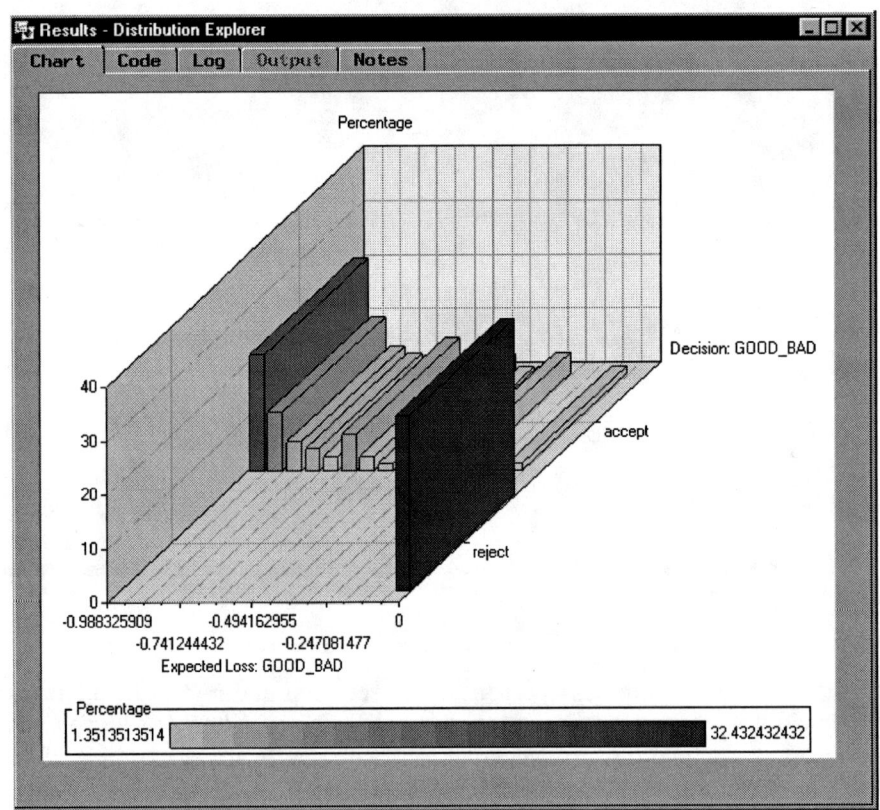

9 After the node finishes running, click Yes in the Message window to display the histogram. To display frequencies on the vertical axis, use the **view** menu to select

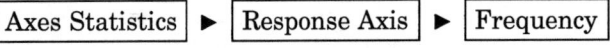

Axes Statistics ▶ Response Axis ▶ Frequency

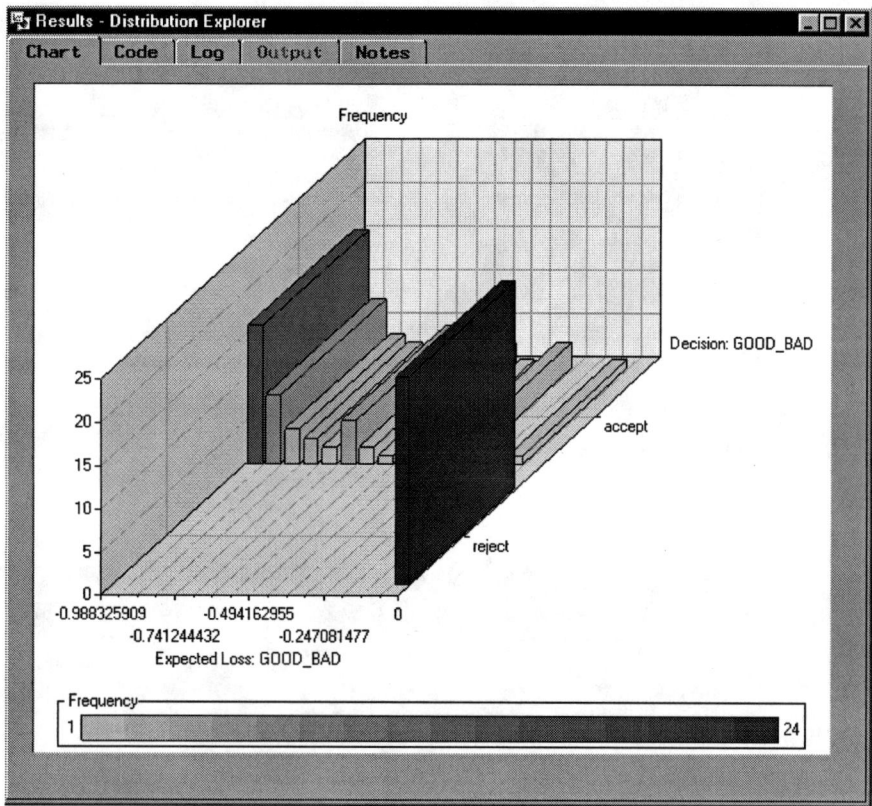

10 Close the Results browser and then close the *Distribution Explorer* node.

---

15. Creating a Score Card of the Good Credit Risk Applicants

To create a score card of the good credit risk applicants, you can use a *SAS Code* node. The *SAS Code* node enables you to incorporate new or existing SAS code into process flows.

1 Add a *SAS Code* node to the data mining workspace.

2 Connect the *Distribution Explorer* node to the *SAS Code* node.

3 Open the *SAS Code* node.

4 The *SAS Code* node provides a macro facility to dynamically reference the data sets and variables. Before you write code to screen for the bad credit applicants, determine the name of the macro variable that references the score data set:

   a Select the Macros tab.

   b Notice that the name of the macro variable that references the score data set is &_MAC_3.

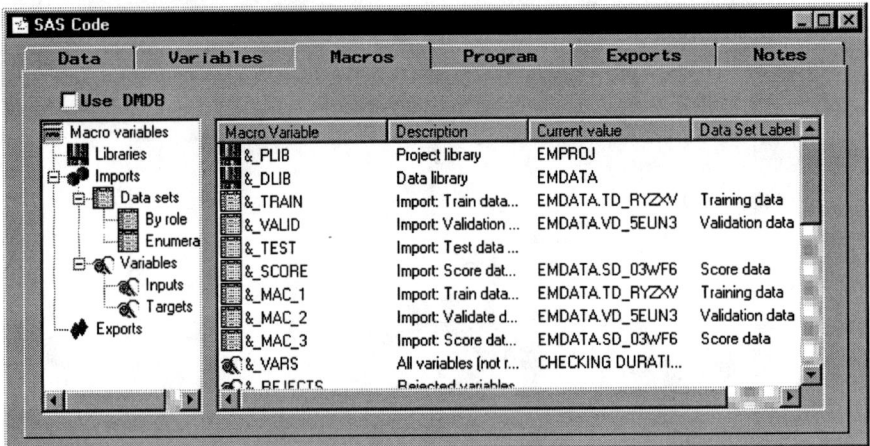

5 Select the Program tab and type the following SAS code:

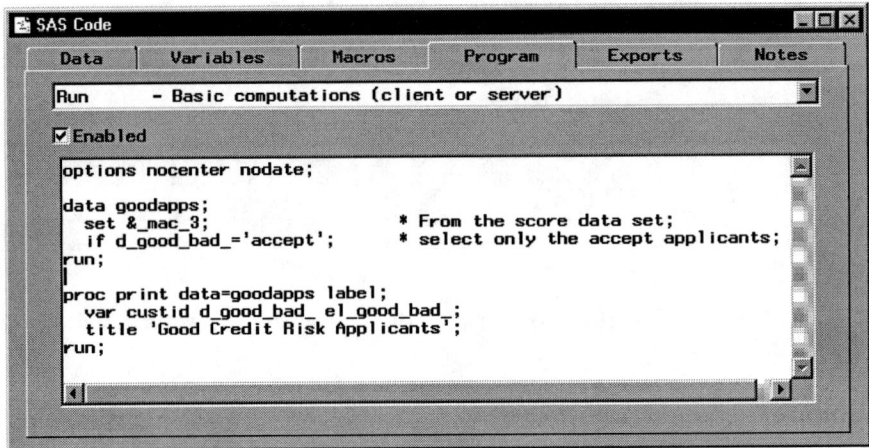

The name of the D_GOOD_BAD_ variable is assigned when you scored the score data set. Make sure you use the correct variable name.

The SAS DATA step reads the observations (customer applicants) from the score data set. The applicants that were assigned to the accept decision are written to the output data set GOODAPPS. These applicants are deemed to be credit worthy.

The PROC PRINT step produces a list report of the good credit risk applicants. The variable CUSTID identifies the good applicants.

6 To run the code, click the Run tool icon.

7 After the code executes, click the [Yes] button in the Message window. Select the Output tab to view the list of good credit risk applicants.

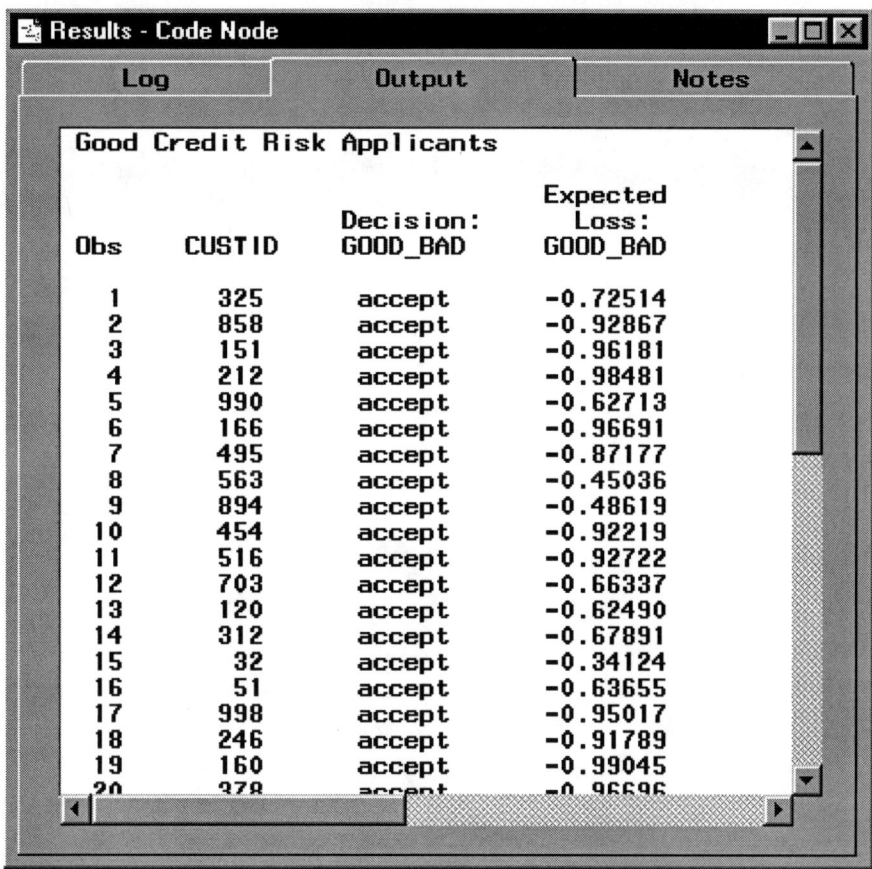

8 Close the *SAS Code* node.

16. Closing the Diagram

When you close the Diagram Workspace, the diagram is automatically saved to the project. You can reopen the diagram and make revisions.

As you apply the production model, you should record and track the results of the model. (Each node contains a Notes tab where you can type and store notes.) At some point as you track the model results, you may determine that you need to use additional data and recalibrate the model to improve its predictive ability.

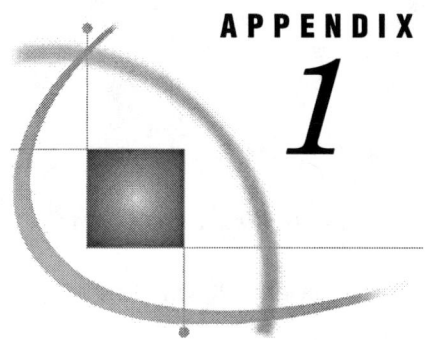

APPENDIX

1

Data Mining Reference List

References

Adriaans, P. and Zantinge, D. (1996), *Data Mining*, Edinburgh Gate, England: Addison Wesley Longman.

Berry, M.J.A. and Linoff, G. (1997), *Data Mining Techniques for Marketing, Sales, and Customer Support*, New York: John Wiley and Sons, Inc.

Bigus, J.P. (1996), *Data Mining with Neural Networks: Solving Business Problems – from Application Development to Decision Support*, New York: McGraw-Hill.

Bishop, C.M. (1995), *Neural Networks for Pattern Recognition*, New York: Oxford University Press.

Breiman, L., Friedman, J., Olshen, R. and Stone, C. (1984), *Classification and Regression Trees*, Belmont, CA: Wadsworth International Group.

Hand, D.J. (1997), *Construction and Assessment of Classification Rules*, New York: John Wiley and Sons, Inc.

Hoaglin, D.C., Mosteller, F. and Tukey, J. W. (1983), *Understanding Robust and Exploratory Data Analysis*, New York: John Wiley and Sons, Inc.

Little, R.J.A., and Rubin, D. B. (1987), *Statistical Analysis with Missing Data*, New York: John Wiley and Sons, Inc.

Little, R.J.A. (1992), "Regression with missing X's: A review," *Journal of the American Statistical Association*, 87, 1227–1237.

Michie, D., Spiegelhalter, D. J., and Taylor, C. C. (1994), *Machine Learning, Neural and Statistical Classification*, New York: Ellis Horwood.

Ripley, B.D. (1996), *Pattern Recognition and Neural Networks*, New York: Cambridge University Press.

Sarle, W.S. (1994a), "Neural Networks and Statistical Models," *Proceedings of the Nineteenth Annual SAS Users Group International Conference*, Cary, NC: SAS Institute Inc., 1538–1550.

Sarle, W.S. (1994b), "Neural Network Implementation in SAS Software," *Proceedings of the Nineteenth Annual SAS Users Group International Conference*, Cary, NC: SAS Institute Inc., 1550-1573.

Sarle, W.S. (1995), "Stopped Training and Other Remedies for Overfitting," *Proceedings of the 27th Symposium on the Interface*.

SAS Institute Inc. (1998), SAS Institute Best Practices Paper, *Data Mining and the Case for Sampling: Solving Business Problems Using SAS Enterprise Miner Software*, Cary, NC: SAS Institute Inc.

SAS Institute Inc. (1999), SAS Institute Best Practices Paper in conjunction with Federal Data Corporation, *Using Data Mining Techniques for Fraud Detection: Solving Business Problems Using SAS Enterprise Miner Software*, Cary, NC: SAS Institute Inc.

SAS Institute Inc. (1995), *Logistic Regression Examples Using the SAS System, Second Edition*, Cary, NC: SAS Institute Inc.

SAS Institute Inc. (1999), *SAS Language: Reference, Version 6, First Edition*, Cary, NC: SAS Institute Inc.

SAS Institute Inc. (1990), *SAS Procedures Guide, Version 8*, Cary, NC: SAS Institute Inc.

SAS Institute Inc. (1995), *SAS/INSIGHT User's Guide, Version 8*, Cary, NC: SAS Institute Inc.

SAS Institute Inc. (1990), *SAS/STAT User's Guide, Version 8*, Cary, NC: SAS Institute Inc.

Small, R.D. (1997), "Debunking Data Mining Myths," *Information Week*, January 20, 1997, http://www.twocrows.com/iwk9701.htm.

Smith, M. (1993), *Neural Networks for Statistical Modeling*, New York: Van Nostrand Reinhold.

Steinberg, D. and Colla, P. (1995), *CART: Tree-Structured Non-Parametric Data Analysis*, San Diego, CA: Salford Systems.

Weiss, S.M. and Indurkhya, N. (1998), *Predictive Data Mining: A Practical Guide*, San Francisco, CA: Morgan Kaufmann.

Weiss, S.M. and Kulikowski, C.A. (1991), *Computer Systems That Learn: Classification and Prediction Methods from Statistics, Neural Nets, Machine Learning, and Expert Systems*, San Mateo, CA: Morgan Kaufmann.

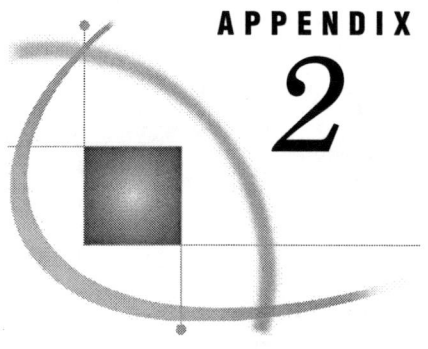

APPENDIX

2

Variable Layout for SAMPSIO.DMAGECR (German Credit Data Set)

SAMPSIO.DMAGECR (German Credit Data Set)

- CHECKING: Status of existing checking account
  - 1: < 0 DM
  - 2: 0 to <200 DM
  - 3: >=200 DM/ salary assignments for at least 1 year
  - 4: no checking account
- DURATION: Duration in months
- HISTORY: Credit history
  - 0: no credits taken/all credits paid back duly
  - 1: all credits at this bank paid back duly
  - 2: existing credits paid back duly till now
  - 3: delay in paying off in the past
  - 4: critical account/other credits existing (not at this bank)
- PURPOSE: Purpose
  - 0: car (new)
  - 1: car (used)
  - 2: furniture/equipment
  - 3: radio/television
  - 4: domestic appliances
  - 5: repairs
  - 6: education
  - 7: vacation
  - 8: retraining
  - 9: business
  - X: others
- AMOUNT: Credit amount
- SAVINGS: Savings account/bonds
  - 1: < 100 DM
  - 2: 100 to < 500 DM
  - 3: 500 to < 1000 DM

- □ 4: >= 1000 DM
- □ 5: unknown/no savings account
- □ EMPLOYED: Present employment since
  - □ 1: unemployed
  - □ 2: < 1 year
  - □ 3: 1 to < 4 years
  - □ 4: 4 to < 7 years
  - □ 5: >= 7 years
- □ INSTALLP: Installment rate in percentage of disposable income
- □ MARITAL: Personal status and gender
  - □ 1: male: divorced/separated
  - □ 2: female: divorced/separated/married
  - □ 3: male: single
  - □ 4: male: married/widowed
  - □ 5: female: single
- □ COAPP: Other debtors/guarantors
  - □ 1: none
  - □ 2: co-applicant
  - □ 3: guarantor
- □ RESIDENT: Date beginning permanent residence
- □ PROPERTY: Property
  - □ 1: real estate
  - □ 2: if not 1: building society savings agreement/life insurance
  - □ 3: if not 1/2: car or other, not in attribute 6
  - □ 4: unknown/no property
- □ AGE: Age in years
- □ OTHER: Other installment plans
  - □ 1: bank
  - □ 2: stores
  - □ 3: none
- □ HOUSING: Housing
  - □ 1: rent
  - □ 2: own
  - □ 3: for free
- □ EXISTCR: Number of existing credits at this bank
- □ JOB: Job
  - □ 1: unemployed/unskilled - nonresident
  - □ 2: unskilled - resident
  - □ 3: skilled employee/official
  - □ 4: management/self-employed/highly qualified employee/officer
- □ DEPENDS: Number of dependents
- □ TELEPHON: Telephone
  - □ 1: none
  - □ 2: yes, registered under the customer's name
- □ FOREIGN: foreign worker
  - □ 1: yes
  - □ 2: no

Glossary

activation function
in the language of neural networks, a mathematical transformation of the net input to yield the output of a neuron.

architecture
in the language of neural networks, a statistical model.

adaptation
in the language of neural networks, the process of estimation and model-fitting.

assessment
determining how well a model computes good outputs from input data not used during training. Assessment statistics are automatically computed when you train a model with a modeling node. By default, assessment statistics are calculated from the validation data set. You can choose to assess the adequacy of a trained model(s) with a test data set. You can compare models using either the Model Manager of a modeling node or the *Assessment* node.

Assessment Graph (Decision Tree)
a graph in the Tree Browser that plots the utility values from the Assessment Table. The red, or lighter, symbols represent the validation data; the blue, or darker, symbols represent the training data. The vertical reference line corresponds to the tree partition highlighted in the Assessment Table.

Assessment Table (Decision Tree)
a table in the Tree Browser that provides a measure of how well the tree describes the data. For a nominal target, the default measure is the proportion of observations correctly classified. For an interval target, the default measure is the average sum of squared differences of an observation from its predicted value. The table displays the assessment for several candidate partitions of the data. In the Assessment Table, one partition is highlighted and the summary statistics for this partition are displayed in the Summary Table in the Tree Browser.

association discovery
the identification of items that occur together in a given event or record. This technique is also known as market basket analysis. Association discovery rules are based on frequency counts of the number of times items occur alone and in combination in the database. The *Association* node is used to perform an association discovery.

back propagation

in the language of neural networks, the computation of derivatives for a multilayer perceptron.

binary variable

a variable that contains two discrete values (for example, PURCHASE: Yes and No). The binary measurement level is automatically set to binary variables in the *Input Data Source* node.

branches

subtrees rooted in one of the initial divisions of a segment of a tree. For example, if a rule splits a segment into seven subsets, then seven branches grow from the segment.

case

a collection of information about one of numerous entities represented in a data set. In SAS System terminology, a case is an observation in the data set.

character variable

a variable whose values can consist of alphabetic and special characters as well as numeric characters.

clustering

the process of dividing a data set into mutually exclusive groups such that the observations for each group are as close as possible to one another, and different groups are as far as possible from one another.

cluster sampling

the process of selecting a sample of groups or clusters from a population. The sample contains all the members of each selected group or cluster. Cluster sampling is useful for transaction data or household data, for example.

combination function

in the language of neural networks, a function that is applied to both inputs and hidden layers that computes the net input to a hidden or output neuron.

cost variable

a variable that is used to track cost in a data mining analysis. You set the cost variable role in the *Input Data Source* node.

data subdirectory

a subdirectory within the project location that contains potentially large files that are created when you run the various process flows in the project. The EMDATA libref is automatically assigned to the data subdirectory.

database

See SAS data set.

data mining database (DMDB)

a SAS data set that is designed to optimize the performance of the modeling nodes. The DMDB enhances performance by reducing the number of passes that the analytical engine needs to make through the data. It contains a meta catalog with summary statistics for numeric variables and factor-level information for categorical variables. All nodes that require a DMDB create one when you run the node. The DMDB node is available if you want to create a DMDB on demand. You may want to create a DMDB with the DMDB node to establish a visual reference for the DMDB in the process flow diagram. The DMDB node also provides the only mechanism for browsing the statistics of a DMDB.

deciles

a division of data into tenths after the data have been sorted by the values of one or more variables. Deciles are usually cumulative, such that the first decile contains the top 10% of the data, the second decile contains the top 20% of the data, and so on.

dependent variable
See target variable.

depth
the number of successive hierarchical partitions of the data in a tree. The initial, undivided segment is at depth 0. Specify a depth value to control how much of the tree to display in a Tree Diagram. See also levels.

diagram
an Enterprise Miner process flow that you interactively create in the Diagram Workspace of the SAS Enterprise Miner window. A diagram is stored in a project. You can create multiple diagrams per project. Diagrams are shareable.

diagram nodes
graphical regions of the Tree diagram and the Neural Network diagram that contain information. For the Tree diagram, a diagram node displays one of three types of information: segment statistics, the names of the variables used to split the segments, or the variable values. For the Neural Network diagram, diagram nodes represent inputs, hidden layers, and targets.

error function
a function that measures how well a neural network or other model fits the training data. The error function is also known as a Lyapunov function or an estimation criterion.

estimation criterion
See error function.

format
a pattern that the SAS System uses to determine how a variable value should be displayed. The SAS System provides a set of standard formats and also enables you to define your own custom formats.

freq variable
a variable that represents frequency of occurrence for other values in each observation. Unlike some SAS procedures, the freq variable can contain noninteger values and can be used for weighting observations. You set the Freq variable role in the *Input Data Source* node.

generalization
to compute accurate outputs using input data that was not used during training.

hidden layer
a layer between input and output in a neural network where one or more activation functions are applied, typically to introduce nonlinearity.

ID variable
an indicator variable. The *Associations* node requires an ID variable for association discovery. You set the ID variable role in the *Input Data Source* node.

imputation
computing replacement values for missing input values. Imputation can be done with the *Replacement* node.

independent variable
See input.

informat
a pattern that the SAS System uses to determine how values entered in variable fields should be interpreted. The SAS System provides a set of standard informats and also enables you to define your own custom informats.

input variable
> a variable that is used to predict the value of the target variable(s). You set the input variable role in the *Input Data Source* node.

internal nodes
> segments of a tree that have been further segmented.

interval variable
> a continuous variable that contains values across a range (for example, TEMP: 0, 32, 34, 36, 43.5, 44, 56, 80, 90, 99, 99.9, 100). You set the interval measurement level to a variable in the *Input Data Source* node.

leaves
> segments of a tree that are not further segmented. The final leaves in a tree are known as terminal nodes.

levels
> successive hierarchical partitions of data in a tree. The first level represents the entire unpartitioned data set. The second level represents the first partition of the data into segments, and so on. See also depth.

libref
> the name that is temporarily associated with a SAS data library.

logistic regression
> a form of regression analysis in which the target (response) variable represents a binary or ordinal-level response.

measurement
> the process of assigning numbers to things such that the properties of the numbers reflect some attribute of the things.

measurement level
> one of several different ways in which properties of numbers can reflect attributes of things. The most common measurement levels are nominal, ordinal, interval, log-interval, ratio, and absolute. Measurement level roles are automatically set to variables in the *Input Data Source* node using the metadata sample.

metadata sample
> a sample of the input data source that is downloaded to the client and is used throughout Enterprise Miner to determine meta information about the data. By default, the meta sample file size is 2000 cases. You can set the metadata sample size in the *Input Data Source* node. The metadata sample is updated with new variables that are automatically created or that you create as you build and run the process flow diagram. The metadata sample is used:
> - to calculate summary statistics, determine the number of variable levels, and determine the frequencies of the variable levels for the active data set in the *Input Data Source* node.
> - to determine hierarchical relationships between variables when running the *Variable Selection* node.
> - as the project data when a remote project is run locally and the data does not exist locally.
> - to determine what cases are filtered in the Automatic Filter window of the *Filter Outliers* node.
> - as the data source to create a bar chart of a variable whenever you select the `View distribution` item for a variable in a node.

model
> a formula or algorithm that computes outputs from inputs. A statistical model also includes information about the conditional distribution of the targets given the inputs.

multilayer perceptron (MLP)
> a neural network with one or more hidden layers, each of which has a linear combination function and executes some nonlinear activation function on the input to that layer.

net input
> the result of the combination function of a neuron. The net input can be transformed by an activation function to yield an output.

neural networks
> a class of flexible nonlinear regression and discriminant models, data reduction models, and nonlinear dynamic systems that consist of an often large number of neurons usually interconnected in complex ways and often organized into layers.

neurons
> linear or nonlinear computing elements in a neural network that accept one or more inputs, compute a function of the inputs, and may direct the result to one or more other neurons. Neurons are also known as nodes or units.

nodes (Tree)
> segments or diagram nodes, depending on context. The terms leaves, nodes, and segments are closely related and sometimes refer to the same part of a tree. See also internal nodes.

nodes (Neural Network)
> See neurons.

nominal variable
> a variable that contains discrete values that do not have a logical ordering (for example, PARTY: Democrat, Republican, other). The *Input Data Source* automatically assigns the nominal measurement level to variables based on the information in the metadata sample. You can also set the nominal measurement level to a variable in the *Input Data Source* node.

numeric variable
> a variable that contains only numeric values and related symbols, such as decimal points, plus signs, and minus signs.

observation
> See case.

ordinal variable
> a variable that contains discrete values that do have a logical ordering (for example, GRADE: A, B, C, D, F). The *Input Data Source* automatically assigns the ordinal measurement level to variables based on the information in the metadata sample. You set the ordinal measurement level to a variable in the *Input Data Source* node.

output
> a variable that is computed from the inputs as a prediction of the value of the target variable.

overfit
> training the model to the random variation in the sample data. Overfit models contain too many parameters (weights), and they do not generalize well.

partition
> dividing the available data into training, validation, and test data sets. You can partition the data with a *Data Partition* node.

perceptron
> a linear or nonlinear neural network with or without one or more hidden layers.

predicted value
See output.

predict variable
a variable that contains the predicted values (outputs) for the target. You set the Predict variable role in the *Input Data Source* node or *Data Set Attributes* node.

profit matrix
a table of expected revenues and expected costs for each decision alternative for each level of the target variable.

project
a collection of Enterprise Miner process flow diagrams. You can create a local or client/server project. Projects are shareable, which means that multiple users can work on the same project simultaneously. Only one diagram can be open within the project at a time. The project contains the .dmp file that corresponds to the project definition, and the various .dmd files, which represent the various diagrams within the project. The name of the .dmp file defines the name of the project. Each project contains a project, data, and report subdirectory.

rejected variable
a variable that is manually excluded from data mining analysis. You set the rejected variable role in the *Input Data Source* node.

project subdirectory
a subdirectory where information for each diagram and its nodes, the target profile, and various registries are stored. In addition, diagram lock (.lck) files are placed here every time a diagram is opened to prevent two users from opening the same diagram at the same time. The EMPROJ libref is automatically assigned to the project subdirectory. A USERS directory exists within the project directory, which contains files that represent the users currently sharing the project.

reports subdirectory
HTML reports generated by the *Reporter* node are stored in this project subdirectory. Each report has its own subdirectory. The name of the subdirectory defines the name of the report.

response variable
See target variable.

root node
the initial tree segment. It represents the entire data set.

root segment
See root node.

rules
definitions of how to split segments of data into subsegments in a tree.

sampling
the process of subsetting the population into *n* cases. You often want to sample the input data to decrease model-fitting time. You use the *Sampling* node to obtain a sample.

SAS data set
descriptor information and its related data values organized as a table of observations and variables that can be processed by the SAS System.

scoring
the process of applying a model to new data to compute outputs. Scoring represents the end result of data mining.

seed

an initial value from which a random number function calculates a random value.

sequence variable

a variable that represents the time span from observation to observation. The *Associations* node requires a sequence variable for sequence discovery. The sequence (time stamp) variable must be recorded on the same scale. You set the Sequence variable role in the *Input Data Source* node.

simple random sample

a sample for which each item in the population has an equal chance of selection.

standard deviation

statistical measure of the variability of a group of data values. This measure, which is the most widely used measure of the dispersion of a frequency distribution, is equal to the positive square root of the variance.

stratified random sample

a sample obtained by dividing a population into nonoverlapping parts, called strata, and randomly selecting items from each stratum.

subdiagram

a collection of nodes in a process flow diagram that are compressed into a single node. The use of a subdiagram may improve your control of the information flow in the diagram.

tabbed dialog box

a window in which you select labeled tabs to access different screens within the window.

target variable

a variable whose value is known in some currently available data (for example, the training data set) but is unknown in some future data sets (for example, the score data set). You typically want to predict the values of the target variable(s) from other known variables. The ordering of the target values determines the event level for class targets. You set target variables in the *Input Data Source* node or *Data Set Attributes* node.

test data

currently available data that contain input and target values that are not used during training, but instead are used for generalization and to compare models. A test data set can be created with the *Data Partition* node. You can also assign the test role to a test data set in the *Input Data Source* node or *Data Set Attributes* node.

training

the process of computing good values for the weights in a model.

training data

currently available data that contain inputs and target values used for model training. A training data set can be created with the *Data Partition* node. You can also assign the training role to a training data set in the *Input Data Source* node or *Data Set Attributes* node.

transformation

applying a function to a variable to adjust its range, variability, or both. Variables can be transformed in the *Transform Variables* node.

tree

the complete set of rules used to split the data into a hierarchy of successive segments. A tree consists of branches and leaves, in which each set of leaves represents an optimal segmentation of the branches above them according to a statistical measure.

Tree Diagram

a graphical representation of (at least) a selected portion of a tree, which may include segment statistics, the names of the variables used to split the segments, and the variable values. Click on the Tree-Ring Navigator to open the Tree Diagram.

Tree Browser

the main analysis window for data segmentation. The Tree Browser contains the Summary Table, Tree-Ring Navigator, Assessment Table, and Assessment Graph.

trial variable

a variable that contains count data for a binomial target, such as the number of responders who responded to a mailing. Some of the trials are classified as events, and the remainder are classified as non-events.

unary variable

a variable that contains a discrete value. The unary measurement level is automatically assigned to unary variables in the *Input Data Source* node.

underfit

training the model to only part of the actual patterns in the sample data. Underfit models contain too few parameters (weights), and they do not generalize well. See also overfit.

units

See neurons.

validation data

data that are used indirectly during training for model selection, early stopping, or for other methods intended to improve generalization. You can also use the validation data set as a selection criterion when running stepwise regression with the *Regression* node. By default, all assessment statistics are calculated using the validation data set. You can create a validation data set with the *Data Partition* node. You can also assign the validation role to a validation data set in the *Input Data Source* node or *Data Set Attributes* node.

variable

one of the items of information that is represented in numeric or character form for each case in a data set.

weights

constants that are used in a model for which the constant values are unknown or unspecified prior to the analysis.

Index

Your Turn

If you have comments or suggestions about *Getting Started with Enterprise Miner™ Software, Version 4.1*, please send them to us on a photocopy of this page, or send us electronic mail.

For comments about this book, please return the photocopy to

SAS Publishing
SAS Campus Drive
Cary, NC 27513
email: yourturn@sas.com

For suggestions about the software, please return the photocopy to

SAS Institute, Inc.
Technical Support Division
SAS Campus Drive
Cary, NC 27513
email: suggest@sas.com

*Welcome * Bienvenue * Willkommen * Yohkoso * Bienvenido*

SAS Publishing Is Easy to Reach

Visit our Web page located at www.sas.com/pubs

You will find product and service details, including

- **sample chapters**
- **tables of contents**
- **author biographies**
- **book reviews**

Learn about

- **regional user-group conferences**
- **trade-show sites and dates**
- **authoring opportunities**
- **custom textbooks**

Explore all the services that SAS Publishing has to offer!

Your Listserv Subscription Automatically Brings the News to You

Do you want to be among the first to learn about the latest books and services available from SAS Publishing? Subscribe to our listserv **newdocnews-l** and, once each month, you will automatically receive a description of the newest books and which environments or operating systems and SAS® release(s) each book addresses.

To subscribe,

1. Send an e-mail message to **listserv@vm.sas.com**.

2. Leave the "Subject" line blank.

3. Use the following text for your message:

   subscribe NEWDOCNEWS-L *your-first-name your-last-name*

   For example: subscribe NEWDOCNEWS-L John Doe

Create Customized Textbooks Quickly, Easily, and Affordably

SelecText® offers instructors at U.S. colleges and universities a way to create custom textbooks for courses that teach students how to use SAS software.

For more information, see our Web page at **www.sas.com/selectext**, or contact our SelecText coordinators by sending e-mail to **selectext@sas.com**.

You're Invited to Publish with SAS Institute's User Publishing Program

If you enjoy writing about SAS software and how to use it, the User Publishing Program at SAS Institute offers a variety of publishing options. We are actively recruiting authors to publish books, articles, and sample code. Do you find the idea of writing a book or an article by yourself a little intimidating? Consider writing with a co-author. Keep in mind that you will receive complete editorial and publishing support, access to our users, technical advice and assistance, and competitive royalties. Please contact us for an author packet. E-mail us at **sasbbu@sas.com** or call 919-531-7447. See the SAS Publishing Web page at **www.sas.com/pubs** for complete information.

See *Observations*®, Our Online Technical Journal

Feature articles from *Observations*®: *The Technical Journal for SAS*® *Software Users* are now available online at **www.sas.com/obs**. Take a look at what your fellow SAS software users and SAS Institute experts have to tell you. You may decide that you, too, have information to share. If you are interested in writing for *Observations*, send e-mail to **sasbbu@sas.com** or call 919-531-7447.

Book Discount Offered at SAS Public Training Courses!

When you attend one of our SAS Public Training Courses at any of our regional Training Centers in the U.S., you will receive a 15% discount on book orders that you place during the course. Take advantage of this offer at the next course you attend!

SAS Institute Inc.
SAS Campus Drive
Cary, NC 27513-2414
Fax 919-677-4444

E-mail: sasbook@sas.com
Web page: www.sas.com/pubs
To order books, call Fulfillment Services at 800-727-3228*
For other SAS business, call 919-677-8000*

* Note: Customers outside the U.S. should contact their local SAS office.

The Power to Know™

Ssas® | SAS Publishing